Fight, Flight, or Faith

How to Survive the Great Tribulation

Fight, Flight, or Faith

How to Survive the Great Tribulation

Charles Cooper

Strong Tower Publishing
Bellefonte, PA
www.strongtowerpublishing.com

We want to hear from you. Please send your comments about this book to contactprewrath@gmail.com.

Copyright © 2008 Charles Cooper

Requests for information should be addressed to:

Prewrath Resource Institute, P.O. Box 783065, Winter Garden, FL 34787

Library of Congress Control Number: 2008942364

ISBN-13: 978-0-9815276-3-5
ISBN-10: 0-9815276-3-9

Cover design by Beth Thomas

All Scripture quotations, unless otherwise indicated, are taken from The NET Bible. Scripture quoted by permission. Quotations designated (NET) are from the NET Bible® copyright ©1996-2006 by Biblical Studies Press, L.L.C. www.bible.org All rights reserved. This material is available in its entirety as a free download or online web use at http://www.nextbible.org/ .

To Scott and Janet

This book is about the possibility of unparalleled suffering. Thank you for the opportunity to watch two people deal with tragic loss. Your circumstances have taught me that no amount of suffering at the hand of Satan and his Antichrist could be any worse than what you have experienced already. It is my hope that I would pass the test as you have.

Acknowledgments

I offer a special word of thanks to the men and women who support the Prewrath Resource Institute with your time, talents, and treasures. Your support makes it possible for me to study and write on a subject that is dear to my heart. For those of you who have financially supported our ministry over the years, this book is as much yours as it is mine. I pray that God will bless and remember you as this book touches the lives of countless people for Jesus Christ. We also acknowledge the special help of Alan Kurschner who helped write and influenced the direction of this book.

Table of Contents

Preface

T he idea that a generation of believers will have to confront the Great Persecution[1], or the unparalleled persecution of Satan and his Antichrist, is troubling for many. Having grown up in a conservative home where the Bible was seen as the Word of God, I know the Great Evacuation[2] before the wrath of God (which, in our home, the Great Persecution was seen to be) was regarded as an incontrovertible fact.

---

[1] This time is also called the "Great Tribulation," but because of the misinformation surrounding this term, we prefer to use the term "Great Persecution" to keep the focus on our argument without distraction.
[2] Commonly called "the rapture."

For many, the notion that you could face the Great Persecution is frightening because of the implications. Naturally, the issue of survival is paramount. No sane person wants to die a horrible and painful death at the hands of truly evil men.

How does one survive? In the last fifteen years, I have seen many people wrestle with this question. Some want to run and hide. Others want to fight. Still others hope to discover some secret way that will honor God, yet leave them pain free.

Unfortunately, we have been culturally equipped to look for the easy way out. I can only say that if a generation of believers will be called to face this season of unparalleled persecution, a "drive-up window" mentality will not get it done. It is high time for God's people to get down to the serious work of studying God's Word. No longer can we depend on teachers to keep everything simple. It is time to move out of the "Gerber" sections of Scripture. It is time for solid meat!

As a good friend of mine would say, "This ain't no kid's game." Survival is simple, but one will not simply survive. Read the rest of these pages to discover what God has done to help that generation called upon to be the *final* generation to face Daniel's Seventieth Week.

Ultimately, survival is not the goal. Faithfulness is!

Introduction

As the title in the fictional series *Left Behind* suggests, there were people *left behind* after the Great Evacuation to face the persecution of Satan and his Antichrist. This book has that audience primarily in mind. It has in mind those who, depending on your view, either will be left behind after the evacuation or who will live through the Great Persecution and be raptured only after the hands of Satan and his Antichrist have resulted in the death of untold millions.

Thus, even if you hold to the pretribulation rapture view, the Great Persecution should concern you! Even if God will remove the first wave of believers before the Great Evacuation (although we think this interpretation gravely incorrect), a second group depicted as "a number which no man could number (Rev. 7:9-12)" will suffer greatly, die, and join the rest of the saints in heaven before the throne of God.

Let's think about that for a moment. "A number which no man could number" constituting people from every nation, tongue, and language? By any measure, that's a lot of people! Do these people have no remedy? Are their futures locked? Is physical survivability impossible for them? At the very least, those who believe that God will remove the Church before the Great Persecution ought to be concerned for those who will be left behind.

The timing of the Lord's *parousia* is a big deal! If it goes the way we believe, the persecution will be terrible for those who are alive to endure it. There are, however, millions in the body of Christ who believe they will miss this terrible time. If they are wrong, they may unexpectedly find themselves facing the wrath of Satan and his Antichrist. If so, those who anticipated and prepared for this persecution will find little consolation in being right.

There has and will no doubt continue to be much debate concerning who will encounter this unparalleled time. Given the awful consequences, it is imperative that we not leave this matter up in the air. For the last several hundred years, men and women have argued their respective positions. Seen by many conservative evangelicals as the most important event yet to occur for believers alive on earth, the Lord's *parousia* holds no small place in their thinking. Judging from the historic success of the *Left Behind* book series, the unprecedented Y2K fiasco, the terrorist attack on the World Trade Center in New York City, and the growing world-wide persecution of Christians, many are crying, "Come, Lord Jesus."

Before the Lord will come, however, it is more than likely that many millions will die at the hands of Satan and his Antichrist. Scripture promises that a final generation of living believers will, one day, be evacuated to heaven in the company of Jesus Christ. This is not our debate. Our debate centers on the *timing* of this event.

Until twenty years ago, two views dominated the debate among rapturists—pre- and posttribulationism. Each camp is made up of committed followers of Jesus Christ. The late Dr. John F. Walvoord was an advocate of the pretribulation view. Having studied at Dallas Theological Seminary myself and spent time in his company, I can testify to Dr. Walvoord's love for God and His Word. "A giant of the faith in modern time" was a fitting title for this man of God. That he believed the Church would be taken before Daniel's final week makes him no less an honorable man.

Dr. Douglas J. Moo, who serves the Lord at Wheaton College, endorses a posttribulation rapture. As Blanchard Professor of New Testament, Dr. Moo has demonstrated an outstanding mind for New Testament exegesis. That Dr. Moo believes Scripture to teach that Christ will return at the end of the Seventieth Week, after the Great Persecution and after the six trumpet and six bowl judgments, makes him no less a committed follower of Christ.

The numbers of faithful followers who hold to each of these positions are many. Given that each view is based on the same passages of Scripture, it is arrogant and illogical to conclude that only one of these positions is absolutely right and the other is absolutely wrong. Logically, it makes more sense that the correct position on the timing of Christ's return is some combination of the two major views.

The question that each position is attempting to answer concerns, not the fact of the rapture, but its timing. Countless hours and gallons of ink have been spent to prove the other position wrong. Scholars continue to search for that one argument that will settle the debate in favor of their respective positions. The result? The discussions have gotten so trivial and the distinctions between words so technical that the average believer cannot follow the arguments.

The price of this continual infighting is a large, uneducated laity convinced that the truth of the matter is beyond their grasp. On the other hand, committed godly men and women support pre- and posttribulationalism with fierce devotion to their positions. For now, the debate is purely esoteric. No real danger exists, for all things continue as before. However, one day *there will be a final generation of humanity to experience the climactic events of this present world order*. The old adage that end-time events "will all pan out" will not be taken so lightly by that generation.

The question before us is this: Can one conclusively demonstrate beyond a shadow of a doubt that a generation of the Church, the Body of Christ, the bride of Christ, God's elect, will face the Great Persecution at the hands of Satan and his Antichrist? Each believer must address this question to his satisfaction before addressing the material in this book: whether to *fight*, to *take flight*, or to *stand in faith* is the right strategy for God's elect.

The passage that holds the key to this debate, in our opinion, is Matthew 24:3-31.[1] However, among rapturists, Matthew 24:1-31 finds little agreement regarding its relationship to the issue of timing. The primary reason is the matter of applicability. While we will not go into the applicability of Matthew 24 to the Church here, we have settled these matters, in our thinking, in our book, *God's Elect and the Great Tribulation: An Interpretation of Matthew 24:1-31 and Daniel 9*. If there is any doubt in your mind that a future generation of God's elect will face the persecution of Satan and his Antichrist, *God's Elect and the Great Tribulation* is must reading.

---

[1] We recognize that there are those who believe Daniel's final week is past, yet would maintain a future rapture as we define it. Partial preterists, among whom R. C. Sproul is counted, would argue this position (see *The Last Days According to Jesus*, R. C. Sproul, for a defense of this position). Our decision to limit this discussion to those who would describe themselves as rapturists in relationship to a yet future fulfillment of Daniel's final week is biased. We see the

question of the applicability of Daniel's final week to New Testament theology as fact. Therefore, we see those who reject a possible future application of the final week as in error. That said, we do allow for the possibility that fulfillment of the final week may not look exactly as we presently understand it. There may be facts we are yet to understand that will add to our understanding and color our present interpretation of this critical text.

Chapter 1

Survival Options: Fight, Flight, or Faith

L et's look at the numbers. Sixty million copies of the *Left Behind* book series were sold. Whether or not you agree with the timing of the Lord's return espoused in this series, a whole lot of people are at least aware that, at the Lord's next appearance, a significant number of people will be left behind. Even those comforted by the thought that they will miss the Great Persecution ought to be, at the same time, somewhat discomforted by the idea that many people who thought they were "Christians" will be left behind.

Given the success of the *Left Behind* series and the increased awareness of approaching end-time events among its many readers, one could reasonably expect a tremendous upturn in evangelism among churchgoing people. Perhaps it will come with time. At present, however, no strategy this author is aware of is in the works to help those left behind. Not to worry. There are many others who believe they will have to face the unprecedented persecution.

Regardless of whether you are among the "left behind" or those yet to be gathered up, surviving the Great Persecution ought to be the ultimate concern of every generation. Regardless of who will face this terrible season, it will not be easy. Should our generation be God's sovereign choice to face it, you need to be *prepared*.

Not everyone agrees as to what preparations one should make to survive. Consider the following three possibilities.

Oscar and Lillian

Oscar and Lillian are married with three children. One day as Oscar read the Scriptures, he became convinced that his generation might be called upon by God to face the Great Persecution during the second half of Daniel's Seventieth Week. By himself, Oscar felt he could easily survive, but with a family, survival would be extremely difficult, particularly if he made no advance preparations.

So Oscar began to think about how to survive. To save his wife and children, he felt that he must learn to fight. Soon after, Oscar learned of a group in Northern Michigan who trained men and women in wilderness survival and guerrilla warfare. He sold his home and moved his family to Michigan to receive this special training. Once there, Oscar began to think about the regions of the United States that are sparsely populated and that would provide good terrain for self-defense.

In Oscar's thinking, once the Great Persecution starts, the first seventy-two hours will be the most critical. Oscar knows that he and his family will have the best chance of survival if as few people as possible are aware of his plans. He maintains a survival pack for each member of his family. The packs (MOLLE packs) contain the most critical items each family member will need.

Each MOLLE pack contains a Snugpak expanda panel along with hydration packs, a Coast Guard survival sleeping bag, rations, and a Gore-Tex parka and pant set. Oscar sees himself alone as carrying the weapons. He has a .223 Rem rifle and a 9mm pistol. His USGI load-bearing vest has three hundred rounds of ammunition, weapons-bearing gear, a USMC-issued KA-BAR knife, a lensatic compass, binoculars, and night vision equipment.

Oscar plans guerrilla raids to take what he needs as the Great Persecution progresses. He hopes to survive without having to kill anyone, but he is fully prepared to kill if necessary. Oscar believes he has a right to defend himself and his family. He understands the Great Persecution to be a reversion to the Jewish age when "an eye for an eye" ruled the day.

Henry and Eula Lee

Henry and Eula are farmers in western Nebraska. They are second-generation believers who recognize that a certain generation of the Church will face the unparalleled horror associated with the Great Persecution. For his part, Henry believes the only possible alternative for believers is to flee to sparsely populated areas and hide until the Lord comes to receive to Himself those who are trusting in Him for physical and spiritual deliverance. This is the essence of the command Jesus gives to those living in Jerusalem when Antichrist takes his seat in a holy place and proclaims himself to be God.

Henry intends to flee from his home, avoiding population centers, to one of the rural low-population areas of a particular Canadian province. Understanding the difficulty of preparing or stockpiling enough food and supplies for three-plus years, he plans to live off the land. His studies have led him to believe that eating foods that do not require cooking is healthier and will allow a small group of people to go undetected in a wilderness area. Following *The Hallelujah Diet*, Henry has made a major effort to identify and be able to recognize those plants that are both tasty and healthy.

To hide, Henry understands that he and his family must limit their waste, keep fires to a minimum, travel no more than a few miles from their hiding place, and limit the number people in their hiding party. Henry believes that he and his family can survive if they can stay warm, stay fed, and remain quiet.

Natural foods high on Henry's list include nuts, vegetables, and wild berries. He knows that dandelions are rich in vitamin A and that pine needles are high in vitamin C. With blackberries and blueberries, Henry can prepare several edible dishes with acorns, hazelnuts, birch bark, and wild carrot root. Henry's bible for wilderness food survival is Peterson's *Field Guide to Edible Wild Plants*. While plants will fill the belly, they do not contain a lot of protein. Therefore, he plans to round out their diet with fish and small trapped animals such as squirrels, raccoons, and rabbits.

William and Gracie

William and Gracie are your average middle-aged Christians who have had the blessed opportunity to study under great teachers of Scripture. They are committed to Scripture and to walking by faith. As such, William believes that the correct response to any situation is faith.

William concludes that God has sovereignly decreed that Satan and his Antichrist will reign on the earth for three-and-a-half years. Therefore, believers should wisely seek to follow God's plan.

Since God is sovereign and knows all things, William believes He has decreed the destiny of all believers. In light of this, William believes that his obligation is to build his faith. He believes that God's will shall be done and the future of Satan and his Antichrist is set. The only unknown is how Gracie and he will perform in the face of unparalleled persecution.

The Choices

Oscar and Lillian plan to fight. Henry and Eula plan to flee. William and Gracie plan to live by faith. These three families have three different strategies. All have the same goal — to survive the Great Persecution until the Lord's trumpet of deliverance blows. Of the three, which strategy has Scripture's sanction? Given the context and conditions that will characterize this period of human history, what is realistic and God ordained?

Chapter 2

Fight: A Problem of Biblical Contradictions

I s there any biblical basis for the plan to fight
Satan and his Antichrist with weapons to stay
alive during the Great Persecution? Will the
biblical injunction of our Lord in Matthew 26:52
fail to be true?

On the night our Lord was to be arrested, Peter
cut off the ear of Malchus, a slave of the high priest
sent to help arrest the Lord. Jesus instructs Peter,
"Put your sword back into its place; for all those
who take up the sword shall perish by the sword"
(Matt. 26:52). Simply stated, anyone who attempts
to stay alive by killing others will himself be killed.

Violence as a means of protection or retribution during the Great Persecution will produce an effect opposite that desired by those who engage in such activity. Behind the Lord's injunction is the recognition that God's sovereign will shall be done. It does not escape our attention that both Peter and Paul found themselves writing to churches embroiled in persecution for their commitment and testimony about Jesus.

The apostle Paul writes to the Thessalonians,

> We know, brothers and sisters loved by God, that he has chosen you, in that our gospel did not come to you merely in words, but in power and in the Holy Spirit and with deep conviction (surely you recall the character we displayed when we came among you to help you). And you became imitators of us and of the Lord, *when you received the message with joy that comes from the Holy Spirit, despite great affliction.* As a result you became an example to all the believers in Macedonia and in Achaia. For from you the message of the Lord has echoed forth not just in Macedonia and Achaia, but in every place reports of your faith in God have spread, so that we do not need to say anything. (1 Thess. 1:4–8, emphasis added)

Not only did the Thessalonians receive the message "despite great affliction," but we learn in

1 Thessalonians 2:14 that their "affliction" came at the hands of their own countrymen. The social pressure of converting to the "followship" of Jesus Christ is described by Paul as "great affliction."

In 2 Thessalonians, Paul again states,

> As a result we ourselves boast about you in the churches of God for your perseverance and faith in all the persecutions and afflictions you are enduring. This is evidence of God's righteous judgment, to make you worthy of the kingdom of God, for which in fact you are suffering. For it is right for God to repay with affliction those who afflict you, and to you who are being afflicted to give rest together with us when the Lord Jesus is revealed from heaven with his mighty angels. *With flaming fire he will mete out punishment on those who do not know God* and do not obey the gospel of our Lord Jesus. (2 Thess. 1:4–8, emphasis added)

Persecution, affliction, and *suffering* are three of the most harsh terms in the New Testament used to depict man's brutality to man. Yet, all are used to describe the circumstances of the Thessalonians in connection with their "followship" of Jesus Christ.

Paul's description of the Thessalonians' response is insightful. He writes, "which you endure." The Greek term for "endure," *anechomai* (ἀνέχομαι), means "to be patient with, in the sense of enduring possible difficulty – 'to be patient with, to have patience.'"[1] The severity of the persecution, affliction, and suffering is not explicitly stated in the text. However, it warrants God's repayment when Jesus Christ is revealed from heaven with His mighty angels.

What is absent is any indication that the Thessalonians were to respond with violence or retribution. In fact, their lack of response in kind only confirms God's justification for including them in His kingdom. The correct responses were *perseverance* and *faith*. "Perseverance" translates *hupomonā* (ὑπομονή) and describes the "capacity to continue to bear up under difficult circumstance — 'endurance, being able to endure.'"[2] The term "faith" (πίστις) has the sense of both faith in the truths concerning God and Christ and faithfulness in maintaining those truths and practices taught by Paul. In effect, the Thessalonians' faith constituted the measuring stick for both their endurance and the basis of that endurance.[3] As we will see, these are the only biblical responses to persecution set forth in Scripture.

The apostle Peter writes in 1 Peter 3:14–16,

But even if you should suffer for the sake of righteousness, you are blessed. And do not fear their intimidation, and do not be troubled, but sanctify Christ as Lord in your hearts, always being ready to make a defense to everyone who asks you to give an account for the hope that is in you, yet with gentleness and reverence; and keep a good conscience so that in the thing in which you are slandered, those who revile your good behavior in Christ may be put to shame.

Peter admonishes his readers to respond to suffering with a *defense*. However, this admonition refers to a defense with words and not with weapons. The term "defense" (*apologia* = ἀπολογία) refers to the content of what is said, not the defense itself. It is defined as "what is said in defense, how one defends oneself."[4] Peter also adds that the correct characterization of one's defense is *gentleness* and *reverence*.

Again, in 1 Peter 4:12-19, we receive more instruction about how believers are to respond to unparalleled persecution:

> Dear friends, do not be astonished that a trial by fire is occurring among you, as though something strange were happening to you. But rejoice in the degree that you have shared in the sufferings of Christ, so that when his glory is revealed you may also rejoice and be glad. If you are insulted for the name of Christ, you are blessed, because the Spirit of glory, who is *the Spirit of God, rests* on you. But let none of you suffer as a murderer or thief or criminal or as a troublemaker. But if you suffer as a Christian, do not be ashamed, but glorify God that you bear such a name. For it is time for judgment to begin, starting with

the house of God. And if it starts with us, what will be the fate of those who are disobedient to the gospel of God? And *if the righteous are barely saved, what will become of the ungodly and sinners?* So then let those who suffer according to the will of God entrust their souls to a faithful Creator as they do good.

Peter begins his exhortation with "do not be astonished." The verb here is *xenizō* (ξενίζω) and means "to receive and show hospitality to a stranger, that is, someone who is not regarded as a member of the extended family or a close friend — 'to show hospitality, to receive a stranger as a guest.'"[5] Literally, in this place we could translate it "stop thinking it a thing alien."[6] He describes the circumstances of his audience: They are a *fiery ordeal.* Literally, the Greek says, "a burning trial." In light of the Old Testament use of this term in the LXX, the idea is that of a smelting furnace.[7] Peter instructs his audience that they are not to treat intense persecution as an unwelcome guest. Rather, he understands the matter to be one of testing, which is not a strange thing for believers.

Peter hopes that his readers will view their circumstances as a privileged participation in Christ's sufferings that will ultimately lead to glory with the Lord at His exultation. Ultimately, none of his readers are to suffer "as a murderer, or thief, or evildoer, or a troublesome meddler." These four terms significantly limit the activities of those not resolved to suffer as good soldiers of Christ.

Peter concludes, saying, "So then let those who suffer according to the will of God entrust their souls to a faithful Creator as they do good." This places a burden on all who suffer to determine whether their circumstances are the will of God. Is it God's will that believers suffer during the Great Persecution? Does Scripture explicitly state how believers are to respond to this terrible event connected with Daniel's final week?

A text that speaks to this specific point is Revelation 13:10. This passage, quoted from *The Greek New Testament*, states:

> If anyone is meant for captivity, into captivity he will go. If anyone is to be killed by the sword, then by the sword he must be killed. This requires steadfast endurance and faith from the saints.[8]

Literally, the Greek says,

13:10a: If (for the sake of argument) anyone for captivity into captivity he goes.

13:10b: If (for the sake of argument) anyone with the sword to be killed, he with the sword to be killed.

One immediately will notice that Revelation 13:10a and 13:10b, when read literally, are rather awkward. The awkwardness results from the absence of a main verb in three of the four main clauses. This absence evidences considerable attempts by early scribes to make sense of these clauses in the original Greek manuscripts. While scholars do not know which combination of reconstructions is best, the sense of the text is not obscured by the irregular grammar. Regardless of what combination of verbs is postulated, saints are advised against fighting their persecutors.

Based on the best scholarship regarding the many possible readings, the best sense of Revelation 13:10 is this:

13:10a: If (for the sake of argument) anyone is destined for captivity, to captivity he goes;
13:10b: If (for the sake of argument) anyone kills with the sword, with the sword he must be killed.

What Revelation 13:10 affirms is that God's elect will experience imprisonment and capital punishment during Daniel's Seventieth Week. Believers' response is not to fight back, but to suffer faithfully. That this is truly the correct interpretation is supported by four facts.

First, Revelation 6:11 affirms that believers will be killed and that God sovereignly knows the precise number of them. Notice the context:

Now when the Lamb opened the fifth seal, I saw under the altar the souls of those who had been violently killed because of the word of God and because of the testimony they had given. They cried out with a loud voice, "How long, Sovereign Master, holy and true, before you judge those who live on the earth and avenge our blood?" Each of them was given a long white robe and they were told to rest for a little longer, until the full number was reached of both their fellow servants and their brothers who were going to be killed just as they had been.

The martyrs in heaven ask, "How long, Sovereign Master, holy and true, before you judge those who live on the earth and avenge our blood?" Simply speaking, they ask God for vengeance on those responsible for their deaths. In response to their question, the martyrs are given white robes and told, "Rest for a little longer, until the full number was reached of both their fellow servants and their brothers who were going to be killed just as they had been." This makes clear that the death of God's elect is not unexpected. God is very much aware of the death of His people. Their number is settled in heaven and will be reached before the martyrs are avenged.

The text also affirms that God is in control, even if His elect are dying. Warren W. Wiersbe writes, "God made clear to these martyrs that their sacrifice was an appointment, not an accident; and that others would join them. Even in the death of His people, God is in control (Ps. 116:15); so there is nothing to fear."⁹

The second fact that supports our conclusion that believers are not to fight but to suffer faithfully is an implied outcome of God's will concerning the limited time for Satan and his Antichrist to rule over the earth. Revelation 13 depicts the second phase of Satan's plan to prevent Jesus Christ from reigning upon the earth as God's choice.

Having failed to prevent Jesus from ascending to heaven to receive the kingdom from God (Satan's first phase), Revelation 13 sets forth Satan's next plan to prevent Jesus from descending from heaven to reign upon the earth. The chapter opens with the reader witnessing the rise of Antichrist from an area east of the land of Israel. The text depicts him as swift, cunning, and agile, with formidable strength and a loud mouth. These are characteristics taken from previous beast kings of Satan's failed policy of preventing the ascension of Jesus to heaven.

Antichrist is raised from death and the world marvels at him and worships Satan because Antichrist is energized by Satan. Antichrist reigns on the earth for forty-two months, during which he blasphemes God, persecutes the elect, and achieves rule over the entire earth. The non-elect will worship him, but the elect will not.

Revelation 13:9 concludes: "If anyone has an ear, let him hear." This argues strongly that believers are John's primary audience. This same phrase occurs as a concluding admonition to all seven churches mentioned in Revelation 2–3. The phrase goes back to the Lord's ministry on earth when He separates those who hear and understand His meaning from those who do not. In Revelation 2–3, the phrase serves to call the churches to the seriousness of their choices in light of the consequences. Therefore, to attempt to resist Satan and his Antichrist is, in a sense, resisting God's will by resisting that which God has allowed. Militarily speaking, resistance will prove futile in any case. Even so, God will allow the survival of those whom He has predestined.

A third factor that supports our conclusion that God's elect are admonished to suffer willingly follows naturally from the fact that there are no scenarios in the book of Revelation that depict "those who dwell on the earth [the wicked]" experiencing imprisonment or capital punishment, with the sole exception of the two witnesses. We recognize that this is an argument from silence. However, the author of the Book of Revelation was imprisoned on Patmos Island (Rev. 1:9); members of the church at Smyrna were imprisoned (Rev. 2:10); the fifth seal depicts martyrs for the cause of Christ (Rev. 6:9); God's two witnesses will be put to death in Jerusalem (Rev. 11:7); saints will be the object of the woman's persecution (Rev. 17:6; 19:2); and capital punishment will be the result for those who refuse to worship or take the mark of the Antichrist. During all of this, there is not one example of God's people experiencing victory over this regime that does not find its primary cause at the hand of God rather than the hands of the saints.

The final fact that supports our conclusion that God's elect are admonished to suffer willingly is that a correct understanding of Revelation 13:10 sees the concluding portion of the verse as confirming that believers are the focus in its opening portion.

John writes, "Here is the perseverance and the faith of the saints." This statement "is a formal, interpretative [sic] conclusion to those preceding statements [sic]."[10] The text relates the response of the elect to the persecution involving the imprisonment and capital punishment by Satan and his Antichrist, as alluded to in Revelation 13:7. Without Revelation 13:10, there would be no indication of God's desired reaction by His people. Given that the persecutors' goal is to cause believers to compromise, God's elect are to face this persecution with endurance and faith.

Revelation 13 describes the program of Satan and his Antichrist to prevent Jesus Christ from returning to set up His kingdom on earth. Their plan will involve the imprisonment and capital punishment of God's elect and highlights the sober fact that God expects submission rather than armed resistance to these villains of all that is good.

Conclusion

Scripture does not give any indication that fighting is an appropriate response to the persecution of Satan and his Antichrist against God's elect. On the contrary, those who will be called upon to face this unexampled time will need another line of defense.

---

[1]Johannes P. Louw and Eugene Albert Nida, *Greek–English Lexicon of the New Testament: Based on Semantic Domains*, electronic ed. of the second edition, 1:307 (New York: United Bible Societies, 1996, c1989).

[2] Ibid.

[3]Charles A. Wanamaker, *The Epistles to the Thessalonians: A Commentary on the Greek Text* (Grand Rapids, Mich.: W.B. Eerdmans, 1990), 218.

[4] Louw and Nida, 1:437.

[5]Louw and Nida, 1:453.

[6]Kenneth S. Wuest, *Wuest's Word Studies from the Greek New Testament: For the English Reader*, 1 Pet. 4:12 (Grand Rapids: Eerdmans, 1997, c1984).

[7] The words "fiery trial" are the rendering of a word used also in the Greek translation of the Old Testament in Proverbs 27:21, which in the A.V. is rendered "a furnace," referring to a smelting furnace where gold is refined. The same word is found in Psalm 66:10, which Vincent translates, "Thou, O God, has proved us: thou hast smelted us, as silver is smelted." The word means literally "a burning," but is used in these passages to refer to a smelting furnace and the smelting process in which gold or silver ore is purified. Kenneth S. Wuest, *Wuest's Word Studies From the Greek New*

Testament:For the English Reader, 1 Pet. 4:12 (Grand Rapids: Eerdmans, 1997, c1984).

[8]Barbara Aland, Kurt Aland, Matthew Black, et al., *The Greek New Testament*, fourth ed. (Federal Republic of Germany: United Bible Societies, 1993, c1979), 657.

[9]Warren W. Wiersbe, *The Bible Exposition Commentary*, "An exposition of the New Testament comprising the entire 'BE' series"—Jkt., Rev. 6:9 (Wheaton, Ill.: Victor Books, 1996, c1989).

[10] G. K. Beale, *The Book of Revelation*, NIGTC (Grand Rapids: William B. Eerdmans Publishing Company, 1999), 705.

Chapter 3

Flight: The Problem of Logistics

A number of God's elect believe that a future generation of saints will face the Great Persecution prophetically depicted in Scripture. They also are persuaded that they can avoid Satan and his Antichrist by fleeing to a place of safety in the unpopulated regions of the world. Naturally, the primary reason for this thinking is self-preservation. This is a powerful motivation. However, before addressing whether this strategy is a biblically justified, we must first answer whether it is a realistic *survivability* strategy.

Some would take Matthew 24:16 as proof that flight to *any* place of safety is workable. The Lord

Jesus, in explaining the severity of the persecution sponsored by Satan and his Antichrist, exhorts those believers living "in Judea [that they] must flee to the mountains" upon the visible appearance of the abomination of desolation in a holy place in Jerusalem. The context indicates that God's elect must flee immediately, not stopping to carry anything with them.

The obvious question is, why? It is because Jesus makes clear that the Great Persecution is coming. By fleeing from Judea, we must conclude that a person will thus rescue himself or herself from that persecution. At this point, we must exercise great care so as not to overtax the text, for it would seem that if one knows that the abomination of desolation is coming, why not leave ahead of time? Or why not make preparations so as not to worry about having to take things when this period begins? In other words, why wait until the last minute?

The idea of fleeing to the mountains for safety is grounded in the Old Testament and illuminates the Lord's instructions to the Jews at the time of the Great Persecution. Genesis 19:17 states, "When they [the angels] had brought them [Lot, his wife and daughters] outside, they said, 'Run for your lives! Don't look behind you or stop anywhere in the valley! Escape to the mountains or you will be destroyed!'" This text emphasizes the need for haste in the face of divine judgment. Similarly, those living in Judea just prior to the abomination of desolation will need to move with haste to save themselves.

To which mountains is the Lord exhorting the Judeans to flee? References to mountains and hills abound in the Bible, with these references numbering approximately five hundred.[1] They refer to both physical phenomena and spiritual symbols.[2] Thus, we must determine which meaning the Lord intends in Matthew 24:16. *The Dictionary of Biblical Imagery* states,

> Mountains and hills have always been significant natural barriers that readily become geographic and political boundaries (Josh. 15:8–16). Extreme conditions make them barren and often sparsely populated. Their unchanging appearance makes them a measure of permanence and solidity. Their natural features (steep slopes, rock outcroppings, sheer cliffs) make them strategic fortress sites (Judg. 6:2). Their many nooks and crannies make them places of hiding and refuge to which to flee.
>
> These physical qualities of mountains give them connotations of being wild, distant and alien to civilization. There are nearly a hundred biblical references to "hill country" (NRSV), implying a region sparsely populated, beyond the pale of what might be considered civilized.

People flee to the hills when their city is destroyed (Gen. 14:10; 19:17).[3]

If physical mountains are the Lord's objective in Matthew 24:16, what will be the options for those living in Judea? There are a number of mountains in close proximity. The short list would include mountains in modern-day Egypt, Jordan, and Syria. Since the purpose of fleeing is to find safety during the Great Persecution, the mountains must be a relatively short distance away.

In Egypt, the Sinai Peninsula is the only option. In northeast Sinai, Egypt, the mountain Hashem El-Tarif towers 8,625 feet. Mount Serbal and Mount Sinai in the south tower 6,750 and 7,496 feet, respectively. Neither provides sufficient cover to protect several thousand people. Jordan's two mountains, Nebo (2680 feet) and Jabal Rum (5,689 feet), are east of Judea, but they would not provide protection for several thousand people, either. The only mountain in Syria that might possibly serve this purpose is Hermon, which stands 9,230 feet. Given the density of the population, the land mass of the mountains, and the possible number of people fleeing, however, no mountain range will, in and of itself, serve as a place of safety.

This supports our contention that the Lord's admonition to believers in Judea focuses on the larger concept of divine safety provided by God. Mountains are a figure of speech. In this case, a metonymy of the adjunct, i.e., the sign is put for the thing signified. *Mountains* (the sign) is put for *safety* (the thing signified). Revelation 12:6, 14 echoes this text. There, God promises to protect the Davidic remnant of Judea by giving them a place of safety.

The important point is to recognize that in the case of both Matthew 24 and Revelation 12, the place of safety is God's design and not man's. There is simply no reason for people to flee the persecution of Satan and his Antichrist for the purpose of hiding. That will be impossible. Perhaps if one person attempted to hide, maybe, but tens of thousands or possibly millions seems highly unlikely. There is no adequate secret or otherwise place to hide that many people for three-plus years anywhere within twelve hours walking or driving distance from Jerusalem. This fact argues strongly for a metaphorical intent to our Lord's instructions to flee in Matthew 24.

Another fact that limits the possibilities of our Lord's intent in Matthew 24:16 concerns modern technology. A spy satellite can observe a target anywhere in the world, whether the target is in a building, traveling along a road, or in the middle of a desert. Satellite pictures are so accurate that they can literally see an object three inches wide on a pavement from miles above the earth. A spy satellite can monitor a person's every movement, even when indoors, deep in the interior of a building, or traveling rapidly down the highway in a car in any kind of weather (cloudy, rainy, stormy). Infrared sensors can negate even the affect of weather. Three spacecrafts in a 35,786km (geostationary) orbit can image all inhabited parts of the Earth and relay the information to almost any computer screen in the world. There is no place to hide on the face of the earth!

The National Reconnaissance Office is the governmental agency responsible for advancements in connection with spy satellites. It is funded through the National Reconnaissance Program, which is part of the National Foreign Intelligence Program. Its budget and personnel are classified. Its headquarters is in Chantilly, Virginia. From what little is known, this organization and its hardware have the specific task of making sure that the rest of the nations of the world obtain very few secrets from the United States military. One of its primary weapons is the spy satellite.

Now into their fifth decade, spy satellites have roamed the skies 100-plus miles above the Earth. It is increasingly clear that with the addition of ground-based technologies to satellite imagery, hiding on Earth is impossible.

Spy satellites travel above Mach 20 as they pass over every spot on the face of the earth twice a day. This capacity gives the CIA and military officers the ability to use satellites to obtain digital snapshots of places of interest in a steady stream of black-and-white images twenty-four hours a day, seven days a week, 365 days a year.

One particular class of spy satellites known as "Keyhole-class" satellites has a resolution of five to six inches, which means they can distinguish an object that small on the ground. Other radar-imaging satellites have a resolution of about three feet. These satellites cannot read license plates, but they can tell whether a car has one. They cannot tell if a person is dressed in a disguise, but they can help an analyst figure out what this person is doing and how many people are with him. These particular satellites cannot hover over an area and provide real-time images, but other "assets" such as unmanned aerial vehicles (also known as drones) can. This alone should give one pause when thinking that it will be possible to go undetected for several years.

Now add this to the equation. The National Geospatial-Intelligence Agency (called The National Imagery and Mapping Agency until 2004) was set up to centralize the manipulation of digital data derived from satellites. This agency has been improving what U.S. officials can "see" through their satellite eyes. Over the past few years, digital data has permitted U.S. intelligence to combine visible light imagery with other imagery to make two-dimensional images multidimensional. The result can be transmitted to users around the world.

This new capacity would prove very effective in tracking people hiding from Antichrist. The development of three-dimensional "virtual reality" animations of land features will expose all potential hiding places in any given place around the world. Unless one is building a hiding place where no one can see, hear, or smell, efforts will be futile. Using such technology, the CIA can search any place on earth, moving street by street, hill by hill, or cave entrance by cave entrance before they arrive on scene. With some newly acquired technology, officers and agents can use a joystick to take a virtual "stroll" through an area long before they arrive.

Drug Enforcement Agency agents have uncovered the vulnerabilities of well-guarded secure locations, such as the hideouts of Cali drug lords, prior to an assault. As early as 1995, DEA and Colombian police carried hard copies of the images when they went after the drug lords so they could determine routes of escape as well as parapets and other high ground they would have to watch during an assault. The technology is only getting better.

NGA now maintains an imaging archive that can be accessed via the closest server. Until the past few years, the imagery, even though the downlink was digital, had to be converted to film because the intelligence community did not have the bandwidth to move it. Now, bandwidth is no longer a problem. There is enough bandwidth to send multi-gigabyte images to wherever they are needed.

Analysts are not limited to satellite imagery. They can add information gathered from other sources to create a more complete three-dimensional image. Photos can be added to the three-dimensional animation of the mountainous or wooded area of any state in America, created mainly from satellite imagery. This will yield a more realistic look for the searchers of those hiding from Antichrist.

Also, an analyst can combine unclassified, low-resolution, multispectral imagery of a high-density wooded and mountainous area (the kind that shows heat and ultraviolet emissions) with high-resolution Keyhole imagery of the same area. Commercially available low-resolution imagery can sense a rise in heat from cooking or other heating requirements, while high-resolution imagery can watch for fuel emissions of various types.

The NGA has become very good at fusing imagery from visible light and radar imaging satellites with imagery from multispectral satellites. The classified radar-imaging satellites (initially code-named "Lacrosse") can see through clouds at night and, to some extent, even see underground. Radar images can be digitally rearranged to create the perspective of seeing the target from all sides, an immense value in the analysis of weapons systems and military installations. Satellites that have infrared cameras, such as the unclassified Landsat, can better detect targets that are camouflaged. It is the combination of multispectral or hyperspectral imagery with visible light imagery (which is used to detect things that each alone cannot detect) that makes hiding impossible.

A newer capability of imagery analysis involves "modeling," or creating three-dimensional computerized models of buildings, ships, planes, and other objects, then combining them to obtain further information. One recent example involved manipulating an image of a North Korean freighter to obtain the ship's internal dimensions, cargo-loading capabilities, and maximum load. Next, the analyst modeled an image of a North Korean Scud missile. By adding details of the ship's history and North Korean missile sales to other nations, the analyst produced a three-dimensional model that could help determine how many missiles were loaded onto a freighter headed for Iran.

The CIA can now use artificial intelligence along with modeling to match a known building to an unknown location. The analyst and computer scientist can take a covertly obtained blueprint, create a digital model of the facility, then "ask" a computer to scan the available imagery to find the completed facility.

The application of these technologies for finding people hiding is limitless, and the technologies are getting better with every passing day.

Conclusion

The obvious conclusion is this: Hiding from Satan and his Antichrist will be next to impossible. Anyone considering flight as an option to survive should reconsider unless he or she is willing to go to Judea and flee with the Jews who are living there at the time of the end (see Chapter 5). This is the only place flight will serve as a legitimate option during the Great Persecution at the end times.

---

[1]Leland Ryken, Jim Wilhoit, Tremper Longman, et al., *Dictionary of Biblical Imagery*, electronic ed. (Downers Grove, Ill.: InterVarsity Press, 2000, c1998), 572.

[2] Ibid.

[3] Ibid.

Chapter 4

Faith: Models of Those Who Shed Blood for Christ

"The blood of martyrs is the seed of the Church."

— Tertullian

S ince the Great Persecution has God's sanction in that He will allow it, *fighting* or *fleeing* will prove poor options to sustain one's life. The biblically mandated option is faith. It is clear that the goal of those who want to fight or take flight is the preservation of physical life. Yet, Scripture continually warns against this very thing.

Salvation in Jesus Christ is meant to remove the fear of physical death.

Fear of the unknown is the primary driver of most people's fear of death. However, for believers, Jesus Christ removes all the unknowns.

Regarding death, the Lord Jesus told His followers,

> A disciple is not greater than his teacher, nor a slave greater than his master. It is enough for the disciple to become like his teacher, and the slave like his master. If they have called the head of the house 'Beelzebub,' how much more will they defame the members of his household! Do not be afraid of them, for nothing is hidden that will not be revealed, and nothing is secret that will not be made known. What I say to you in the dark, tell in the light, and what is whispered in your ear, proclaim from the housetops. Do not be afraid of those who kill the body but cannot kill the soul. Instead, fear the one who is able to destroy both soul and body in hell. Aren't two sparrows sold for a penny? Yet not one of them falls to the ground apart from your Father's will. Even all the hairs on your head are numbered. So do not be afraid; you are more valuable than many sparrows." (Matt. 10:24–31)

From this text, we can discern several principles for how believers should respond to the persecution of Satan and his Antichrist. First, the Lord informs His disciples to expect fully to suffer to the same degree that He did (see Luke 12:4). We know that His suffering ultimately led to His death. Therefore, dying is nothing other than suffering the ultimate fate of those who follow Jesus Christ.

That followers of Christ are destined to suffer to some degree is certain. At the least, all agree that we are to suffer in our denial of the flesh. However, the Lord told His disciples directly that they would have tribulation (θλῖψιν = *thlipsis* [tribulation]) in the world (John 16:33). This is not spiritual tribulation, but physical. Both the apostle Paul and the churches he founded continually were persecuted by both religious leaders and government officials. It is a fact that believers can take for granted.

A careful evaluation of Luke/Acts demonstrates that this was true in the lives of the Lord's followers. One author remarks, "Luke emphasizes the church's task of preparing Christians to endure in the time of persecution (which is characteristic of Luke's own time)."[1] Luke's retelling of the Olivet Discourse blends the destruction of the temple and the eschatological return of Jesus Christ. As such, the persecution of the disciples indicates fulfillment of the Lord's prophetic words.

Scott Cunningham's conclusion from his study of Luke/Acts regarding the theme of persecution follows:

(1) Persecution is part of the plan of God.
(2) Persecution is the rejection of God's agents by those who are supposed to be God's people.
(3) The persecuted people of God stand in continuity with God's prophets.
(4) Persecution is an integral consequence of following Jesus.
(5) Persecution is the occasion of the Christian's perseverance.
(6) Persecution is the occasion of divine triumph.[2]

Each generation of the Church has faced a degree of persecution, but the final generation will face the worst persecution of all. If called upon, are we prepared to stand?

Second, certain information we receive from God has the potential to cause hatred by the world (v. 27). What God shares with His people in privacy, they are to share openly. What God shares in the ear of His people, they are to preach from the housetops. Clearly, the Lord expects His people to share the truth if and when a situation demands it, even if doing so would cause the death of the messenger.

Third, soul death is to be feared, but not physical death (v. 28). For those who follow

Jesus Christ, a proper perspective is necessary regarding death. Destruction of the body is all that those of this world can do to a believer. However, God is able to destroy both body and soul.[3] This is a question of loyalty. These are the choices we have: self-preservation in this world at the expense of possible divine judgment; and disapproval or physical death in this world but eternal preservation in the world to come. Fear is good, but only if God is the object of that fear.

Regarding the persecution that believers are inevitably to experience in the world, the Lord instructs His followers never to fear the world, not even once. Most would agree that the painful suffering that comes with persecution (pain that may even bring about death) is frightening, but it is God's care for us that must motivate us to stand strong, even in the face of such persecution.

What follows are two faith models: a first-generation Christian, Stephen, and a last-generation group of believers, the fifth-seal martyrs. There are similarities and differences between them. I believe that an understanding of both will provide us with insight for our own lives, particularly if God calls us unto this ultimate sacrifice to His glory.

A Biblical Model: Stephen, Christ's Martyr

The martyrdom of Stephen was pivotal for the early church. He was the first Christian martyr and is known only from the Acts of the Apostles

(Chapters 6–7). His gifts of faith, wisdom, and power were recognized by the Jerusalem church when it delegated him along with six others to the responsibility of administering food to both Greek-speaking and native Hebraic widows. But service was not his only act of worship. He was a "man full of God's grace and power, [and] did great wonders and miraculous signs among the people." These wonders caught the eye of Jewish leaders who "began to argue with Stephen, but they could not stand up against his wisdom or the Spirit by whom he spoke." Notice that he did not flee from defending his convictions; nor did he prepare for an ensuing physical confrontation. Stephen used wisdom, which is truth guided by the power of the Spirit. This is what our Lord promised us during His earthly ministry. This is the *confidence* that the Church should have during the Great Persecution. I am sure that some believers within Stephen's own church might have opposed his boldness and tried to suggest that he be more circumspect. But his zeal, wisdom, and empowered faith would have none of that.

What was the response of the Jewish leaders to Stephen's wisdom? Did they want to learn more of what he had to say? Did the miracles he performed spawn any curiosity about the power behind them? Sadly, this was not the case. The response from prideful men blinded by their encrusted tradition was not unexpected. "They secretly persuaded some men to say, 'We have heard Stephen speak words of blasphemy against Moses and against

God.'" Moreover, because their own opposition to Stephen was not enough, "they stirred up the people and the elders and the teachers of the law." Then they became physical and "seized Stephen" and solidified their case against him and "produced [more] false witnesses." Yet, that was not the worst. After Stephen gave his case for God's redemptive plan, the Jewish leaders dragged him out of the city and began to stone him.

What was Stephen's reaction to this hostility? Did he say to them, "Wait a minute, there must be some misunderstanding"? Did he attempt to mollify the situation or speak in pragmatic terms so as to think of his own temporal needs? Did he seek an acquittal? We are told that when he was brought to the Sanhedrin, "his face was like the face of an angel." This was a man full of faith and the Holy Spirit, so he could not have been full of fear and anxiety. This was a man who did not wait until the last minute to prepare for this spiritual ordeal. He was already a servant of the Lord Jesus on a daily basis.

Stephen's defense included a panorama of God's redemptive activity throughout Israel's history, culminating in the condemnation of the then-present Jewish leadership who "betrayed and murdered" the Messiah. As Stephen saw the furious response of the leaders and knew that his fate had been sealed, the text says,

Stephen, full of the Holy Spirit, looked up to heaven and saw the glory of God, and

Jesus standing at the right hand of God. 'Look,' he said, 'I see heaven open and the Son of Man standing at the right hand of God.'

To Stephen, seeing his Lord as an advocate welcoming him to Himself at this critical moment confirms that his testimony is true and faithful. Earthly injustice serves as vindication for heavenly justice. Jesus was faithful to the promise, "I tell you, whoever acknowledges me before men, the Son of Man will also acknowledge him before the angels of God." For Stephen, it did not matter what happened to his earthly body. It was negligible compared to what is of so much more significance—the good news of the work of God in his Son Jesus.

As he was being stoned, Stephen's attitude did not change. The text says he prayed, "'Lord Jesus, receive my spirit.' Then he fell on his knees and cried out, 'Lord, do not hold this sin against them.'"

In this ordeal, did Stephen flee? Did he fight? What was his weapon against such injustice and hatred? It was faith. It was not ordinary faith, but faith that is truly Spirit-empowered, that is mature, and that says, "World, you can throw anything at me, and I will respond with love and faithfulness to my Lord." This is the kind of faith that will be necessary during the testing that will come upon the Church during the Great Persecution. This is the kind of faith that you will need if God calls this generation of the Church to encounter Antichrist and his spiritual and physical genocide.

Stephen's example also demonstrates how God's all-wise decrees bring about His all-good purposes in the spread of the gospel. For the embryonic church, this persecution would take the gospel by means of other believers "as far as Phoenicia, Cyprus and Antioch." Yet, Stephen was not aware that God would use his martyrdom for such a shotgun-blast pattern of evangelism. His concern was faithfulness to God and to testify to the victory of the Son over death and sin.

Don't be surprised, Christian, when they bring false accusations about you, just as they did against Stephen. Don't be surprised when they refuse to listen to biblical reasoning as they did with Stephen. Do not flinch, as Stephen did not flinch. Stay true to our Lord, even in the midst of stones being hurled at you, for Christ will be with you, and you will know His sufferings. The Apostle Paul writes,

> I want to know Christ and the power of his resurrection and the fellowship of sharing in his sufferings, becoming like him in his death. (Phil. 3:10)

A Prophetic Model: Fifth-Seal Martyrs

> When he opened the fifth seal, I saw under the altar the souls of those who had been slain because of the word of God and the

testimony they had maintained. They called out in a loud voice, "How long, Sovereign Lord, holy and true, until you judge the inhabitants of the earth and avenge our blood?" Then each of them was given a white robe, and they were told to wait a little longer, until the number of their fellow servants and brothers who were to be killed as they had been was completed. (Rev. 6:9-11 NIV)

The Book of Revelation demonstrates God's absolute sovereignty over injustice. It is not simply that "God is in control," but that all that happens — good *and* evil — unfold in His providence according to His all-wise and all-good purposes. For whatever unknowable reasons, God has ordained that the culmination of this age and the inception of the next will unfold in the dramatic, sober, and awesome events revealed in the last book of the Bible. It will all come to pass, just as He says.

The Book of Revelation reveals victory. Divine victory implies opposition, wrongdoing, and purpose. This is vividly seen as John sees under the altar in heaven the martyred souls of "those who had been slain because of the word of God and the testimony they had maintained." A recurring theme in Revelation is the exhortation for believers to stand firm against worshiping the beast's (Antichrist's) image. Simply stated, there will be many temptations during the Great Persecution: worshiping the beast's image; participating in the mark of the beast in order to purchase and sell goods; and giving up faith and going along with that future system in order to function in society.

We are also told in Revelation 12:17 that Antichrist will be *actively* pursuing believers. *Then the dragon was enraged at the woman and went off to make war against the rest of her offspring – those who obey God's commandments and hold to the testimony of Jesus.* Consequently, the beast's hatred for God's faithful will result in souls under the altar. This is a frightening proposition, but the alternative is far worse. The eternal consequences for unfaithfulness are unmistakably clear.

> And the smoke of their torment rises forever and ever. There is no rest day or night for those who worship the beast and his image, or for anyone who receives the mark of his name." This calls for patient endurance on the part of the saints who obey God's commandments and remain faithful to Jesus. (Rev. 14:11–12 NIV)

But rewards for staying true to Christ are promised.

> I saw thrones on which were seated those who had been given authority to judge. And I saw the souls of those who had been beheaded because of their testimony for Jesus and because of the word of God. They had not worshiped the beast or his image and had not received his mark on their

foreheads or their hands. They came to life and reigned with Christ a thousand years. (Rev. 20:4 NIV)

During this intense time of testing, there will be no proverbial fence on which to sit. The martyred souls will know this first hand. Those who hesitate, question, or rationalize during the Great Persecution will quickly find themselves in apostasy and be at risk for eternal perdition. Conversely, those who trust the Word of God (God's commandments) and maintain their testimony (loyalty to Christ) will find that their suffering is temporal but their reward is eternal.

We learn from John's vision that the fifth-seal martyrs "called out in a loud voice." The anguish in their cry was emphatic—as would be expected after the unspeakable injustice that ended their earthly lives. What follows is the only prayer of supplication we find in the Book of Revelation. "How long, Sovereign Lord, holy and true, until you judge the inhabitants of the earth and avenge our blood?" This unique prayer should, in our estimation, be seen as pivotal in the Book of Revelation. Notice that the souls are asking *when* God will avenge their blood. They are not asking how He could do this to them, because believers cannot be subjected to God's Day-of-the-Lord wrath (1 Thess. 5:9).

Two significant observations: (1) These faithful martyrs recognize that their death is not the result of God's wrath, and (2) they understand that God's wrath is still in the future. Some have wrongly assumed that the first six seals contain God's wrath during the Day of the Lord. This is not the case. The wrath of God begins at the opening of the seventh seal, which contains the trumpet judgments. These, in turn, are followed by the bowl judgments. (See my explanation in the endnote explaining that the first six seals are not God's wrath).[4]

How long, the souls ask, will God take before He vindicates the injustice of wrongful death? They address God as "Sovereign Lord," for these souls understand that this evil is within the all-good, all-wise providence of God. In short, their martyrdom was not purposeless. They are not asking God, "Is it in your power to vindicate this injustice?" No! They ask *how long*, knowing full well that God rules with innate omnipotence, far beyond the lesser powers of evil. He is not only sovereign, but holy and true. These qualities are diametrically opposed to what Antichrist stands for: wickedness and falsehood.

When the souls ask God when He will "judge the inhabitants of the earth and avenge our blood," they are not asking out of some personal vindictiveness. Rather, their acknowledgment of God's being "holy and true" reveals their eagerness for satisfying divine justice. If God is to be feared as true and holy, evil must be dealt with and not left undone. This is the activity of God: "Do not take revenge, my friends, but leave room for God's wrath, for it is written: 'It is mine to avenge; I will repay,' says the Lord" (Rom. 12:19 NIV).

I need to pause for a moment to expand on this latter truth. If God calls our generation to experience the Great Persecution, there will be Christian friends, relatives, immediate family, and even we ourselves who may suffer martyrdom. This suggests another possible spiritual test during such a time. It can be natural to become embittered and vengeful if these events occur close to home. *Stand firm and keep your heart soft.* Do not take revenge, for that is the Lord's work. Rather, "Love your enemies and pray for those who persecute you" (Matt. 5:44 NIV).

Before the souls are given an answer as to the duration of time before God avenges their martyrdom, they are given a "white robe." There is some discussion of what the white robe denotes. It could mean "purity," "worthiness," "victory," or "reward of glory." Some have even suggested that it indicates the souls are given their glorified bodies early (see also Rev. 7:9, 13, 14; 19:8). Whatever the exact meaning, it gives assurance to these saints as "they were told to wait a little longer, until the number of their fellow servants and brothers who were to be killed as they had been was completed." They have cried out to their Sovereign Lord. Now they receive an answer: a little while longer. God is sovereign over time itself (c.f., Acts 17:26, 31; 2 Peter 3:8).

What is the purpose of this extended time? In His absolute wisdom, God has determined the exact number of believers to suffer martyrdom. This further demonstrates God's sovereignty.

The passage seems to indicate two separate groups of people: "fellow servants" and "brothers." Some have suggested that "brothers" indicates Jewish believers and "fellow servants" indicates Gentile believers. This may be too subjective for us to ascertain. Further, the Greek construction "and [*kai*] ... and [*kai*]" can indicate one group as a whole, with the second phrase as explanatory of the first. In any case, they are all saints ordained for martyrdom. Once that is brought about, the cup of God's wrath will be poured out.

Recently, there has been a spate of "devotional" commentaries on Revelation. This is not a bad phenomenon in itself. We are to glean spiritual truths and learn to exalt our great King Jesus from what has been revealed to us in the last book of the Bible. What is unfortunate is that, in some of these commentaries, there is a tacit (sometimes explicit) admission of skepticism in relation to the overall framework and exegetical rigor of Revelation. What is often communicated to readers is that what is "spiritual" is more important than the events that are portrayed. This is a false dichotomy. Revelation is a prophecy. What is the basis for spiritual truth? It is that which is grounded in a future reality. Revelation 1:3 states, "*Blessed* is the one who reads the words of this *prophecy*, and blessed are those who hear it and take to heart what is written in it, because the time is near" (emphasis added). This prophecy is for *you*, beloved.

The Book of Revelation should not be read from a distance — that is, as a book having little or no relevance for your life. Rather, it is imperative (as Jesus exhorts) to read it with the understanding that these events can occur in any generation of the Church. If that is the case, a fresh reading of the fifth-seal martyrs' text should jolt a believer with a sober desire for readiness. In other words, and not to sound sensational, one of those souls that John sees under the altar could very possibly be *yours*. They are not some abstract group, but the living souls of believers who were slain for their faithfulness to the Lord Jesus Christ. They endured real suffering before entering into their rest.

Martyrdom: the Glorifying End of Faith

Commenting on believers who die for Christ, John Piper says,

> The noble army of martyrs are praising God with us this morning because they all said, "For me to live is Christ and to die is gain." They all said, Christ is worth more than life. Christ is worth more than falling in love. Christ is worth more than marrying and having children. Christ is worth more than seeing my children grow up and become independent. Christ is

worth more than making a name for myself. Christ is worth more than finishing my career. Christ is worth more than the dream spouse and the dream house and the dream cruise and the dream retirement. Christ is worth more than all my unfinished plans and dreams.

All the martyrs said, "It is better to be cut off in the midst of my dreams, if I might gain Christ." The stories of martyrs press a question on us: Do we love Christ more than we love life?[5]

Believer, can you say that Christ is worth more than all these temporal possessions and goals? This is not a peripheral question, but one of existential import, even as to what it means to be a Christian. Martyrdom implies that something has more worth than life, and in Christian martyrdom, Christ is that something. Further, one must be of the mindset that we do not choose martyrdom, but God chooses it for us. Particularly is this the case during the Great Persecution. Pray that if God wills this in your life, you will be prepared to give your life for the infinite worth that is Christ.

We are not alone. The greatest of all martyrs was our Lord Himself. He not only testified by word and deed in His life, but also perfectly in His death. Any person who dies *for* Jesus dies *with* Jesus — in imitation of Him.

Conclusion

Of the three options some have contemplated for surviving the persecution of Satan and his Antichrist—fight, flight, or faith—it is our conviction that physically fighting against Satan is not an option. Fleeing with the Jews living in Judea during the specific period in question is the only possible path to physical survival during this period. All other attempts to flee will prove futile. The last option is standing in faith on the promises of God. In the following chapters, we shall examine each of these options in detail.

First, we shall determine whether moving to Judea and fleeing with knowledgeable Jews is realistic. The remaining portions of the book will take an in-depth look at faith to assess how one might develop his or her faith to stand in quiet confidence as Satan and his Antichrist take their best shot.

---

[1] Scott Cunningham, *'Through Many Tribulations': The Theology of Persecution in Luke–Acts* (Englando: Sheffield Academic Press, 1997), 25.

[2] Ibid., 337–338.

[3] "Destroy" here does not mean "annihilation," but the eternal punishment to which "in hell" refers.

[4] First, the cosmic disturbances of the sixth seal announce God's wrath upon the ungodly, as prophesied by Joel: "I will show wonders in the heavens and on the earth, blood and fire and billows of smoke. The sun will be turned to darkness and the moon to blood *before* the coming of the great and dreadful day of the LORD" (Joel 2:30–31 NIV). Second, both the response from the martyrs at the fifth seal and from the ungodly at the sixth seal reveal that God's wrath is soon to come—they had not

already viewed it in the past. Third, the fact that in the seventh chapter of Revelation there are two groups of people, one being sealed and the other being delivered just before the seventh seal is opened, suggests strongly that they are being sealed and delivered from something looming that will come upon the whole world. Fourth, the nature of the events comprising the first four seals is marked by a series of "common" yet intense calamities (war, famine, etc.) carried out by horsemen. All this is in contrast to the opening of the seventh seal (with its supernatural judgments) that represents the decreed wrath of God that is mediated directly by angels via the trumpet and bowl judgments against the ungodly. Also note that a fourth of mankind is not killed at the fourth seal. Only "power over a fourth of the earth" is given. Fifth, the first five seals in Revelation 6 parallel Jesus' teaching about this being only the "beginning of birth pangs" in Matthew 24:5–8. Sixth, the fifth seal is not God's wrath because it specifically speaks of the martyrdom of believers—all of whom are exempted from God's wrath.

[5] Sermon by John Piper, "The Noble Army of the Martyrs Praise Thee," May 23, 1993.

Chapter 5

Plan B: An Easy Way to Survive

The survivability of God's elect during the Great Persecution will be in accord with God's sovereign will. Revelation 6:11 makes clear that the physical death of God's elect during this period is no secret to God. How many believers will die is not clear. Therefore, we must trust God that "all things will work together for good."

As stated earlier, in the following pages, *we shall discuss two avenues for survivability* if God so wills it. The first requires only that one believe a particular promise of God concerning those living in Jerusalem and Judea in the days immediately preceding the abomination of desolation. The second requires faith in all the promises of God regarding spiritual warfare and the believer's authority. We shall discuss the easy way first, then turn our attention to the road less traveled.

Plan B: Follow the Jews

Both Matthew 24 and Revelation 12 make clear that a group of Jews living in Israel during Daniel's final week will receive divine protection by being placed in protective custody for 1,260 days (forty-two months). Also, by fleeing to the mountains/desert, either that same group or another group of Jews is ensured survival throughout Daniel's Seventieth Week. Scripture does not explain in detail how God will protect these people. We simply have God's promise that He will, and that is enough.

Revelation 12:6 and 14 indicate that a group of Jews (the woman) will receive God's protection for the forty-two months that comprise the second half of Daniel's Seventieth Week.[1] This unsaved remnant will receive God's eternal salvation at the end of 1,260 (forty-two months) and enter into God's temporal kingdom in physical bodies. Believers can attach themselves to this group until the ethereal reunion of the righteous at the beginning of the Lord's *parousia*. God promises special care for those who are kind to the Jews during the period following the evacuation of God's elect to heaven. Compassion shown to them in their time of need will secure one's entrance into the temporal (millennial) kingdom in a physical body.[2]

Anyone worried about surviving the Great Persecution may want to consider moving to Jerusalem as soon as he or she is aware that the Seventieth Week has begun. In Egypt during the great exodus, those Egyptians willing to attach themselves to God's people were saved. So, too, will those who are among the Jewish people in the days just before the final three-and-a-half years of Daniel's final week. Matthew 24:16 warns those living in Judea to flee to the place of safety that God will provide in the wilderness.

That one's relationship to the Jews during the final period will prove extremely beneficial has support in Matthew 25, to which we now turn our attention.

Matthew 25:31–46: An Exposition

Matthew 25:31–46 details the Lord's instruction concerning the sheep and goat judgment of the nations that follows the battle of Armageddon and occurs just prior to the beginning of the temporal (millennial) kingdom. Notice:

> When the Son of Man comes in his glory and all the angels with him, then he will sit on his glorious throne. All the nations will be assembled before him, and he will separate people one from another like a shepherd separates the sheep from the

goats. He will put the sheep on his right and the goats on his left.

Matthew began the primary eschatological section of his gospel (Chapters 24–25) by refocusing the Lord's Olivet teachings to answer a question regarding His *parousia* and the end of the age. A comparison of the questions as they appear in the gospels of Mark and Luke reveals that, in the disciples' two-part question, Matthew made a significant change in reporting the second part. Our study (which can be found in our book: *God's Elect and the Great Tribulation*) reveals that Matthew reformulated the question for a purpose. While the parallel tellings in Mark and Luke focus on the destruction of the second temple, Matthew recognized the dual nature of the fulfillment of this prophecy and refocuses the material to emphasize the end-times fulfillment—the time immediately preceding the setting up of the kingdom of God on earth by the King of the Jews.

This same emphasis occurs in the thirteenth chapter of Matthew's gospel. In material unique to the writer, Matthew indicates that the end of the age is the harvest, the great separation of the righteous and the wicked. This final division is about to occur and will bring about the separation of the wheat/tares, the sheep/goats, the righteous/wicked, or the sons of the kingdom from the sons of evil. This event is necessary prior to God's temporal kingdom coming down to earth.

It is during this particular period that God promises the final salvation of the nation of Israel. We are correct to assume that the fulfillment of Isaiah 66:18-20 is complete. At this time, all the Jews who survive the Day of the Lord and were not living in the land of Israel have been brought home by the Gentiles. Those who brought them and any who were particularly caring during the final days of Daniel's Seventieth Week until Armageddon will receive their special reward: entrance into the temporal (millennial) kingdom in physical bodies.

Having finished the parable of the talents, which explains the basis of God's system of rewards regarding positions of honor in the temporal kingdom, Matthew now must explain the final and ultimate separation of those who are not citizens of the nation of Israel—the Gentiles. From the beginning of Matthew's eschatological discourse, he had as one of its purposes to explain the great separation at the end of the age (Matt. 24:3). We discern the magnitude of this event by the number of angels present—all of them. Verse 31 indicates that the King is ruling before the kingdom actually starts. However, housekeeping requires the removal of all who offend prior to the actual beginning of the temporal kingdom (John 3:5).

The Lord shall "sit on His glorious throne," having arrived from heaven with His angelic accompaniment. As Matthew relates this information, there is no statement as to the whereabouts of the bride of Christ who was removed to heaven *at least* seven to eight and a half months earlier. Also, there is no indication that the angels themselves are involved in a gathering of the people. Furthermore, there is no mention of the Lord fighting at Armageddon. That matter has faded into the background as the final act of this age is about to occur.

The Great Separation

The goal of the ages has been that "all the nations will be gathered before Him." *Will be gathered* is passive voice, which suggests that the nations are drawn together, although not necessarily by their choice. The text does not tell the reader where this gathering takes place. After the trumpet and bowl judgments, the earth is in pretty bad shape. Since the destiny of the sheep is the earth where their Lord will rule, and Jerusalem is the geographic destiny of the Son of Man from heaven, we can only assume that the gathering will take place somewhere close to the land of Israel near Jerusalem.

To appreciate this passage fully, the reader must understand that the Jewish people are not included in this gathering because their judgment and restoration is already complete by this time. It is the behavior of the Gentiles toward the Jews that will distinguish the two groups. Gentiles who befriend and help Jews will find grace from God to enter the temporal kingdom in physical bodies.

However, before we look at this fact in detail, we must answer the question: "What is the basis of the claim that ethnic Israel is not included in the sheep and goat judgment?[1]

Matthew 25:32 indicates that "all the nations will be gathered before Him." This would seem to indicate that Israel is among this group about to be judged. However, the phrase τὰ ἔθνη (*ta ethna* = "the nations") "is generally employed in the New Testament to denote *Gentiles* as distinguished from Jews."[3] This particular phrase occurs twenty-five times in the Gospels (Matthew 12; Mark 4; Luke 9). Fifteen of the plural form *ethna* (ἔθνη) appear apart from the Lord's instructions about the end times and clearly refer to Gentiles only.[4]

In the Gospel of Matthew, with reference to the Great Commission, Matthew records that the Lord instructed His Jewish disciples to make disciples of the Gentile nations (Matt. 28:18–20). The Lord indicates that this will require them to "go," which implies movement away from their homes to where the Gentiles are. Matthew 24:14 explains that the gospel of the kingdom (of God)[5] will be preached to the Gentiles. Because Jesus had already preached the message to the Jews,

---

[1] Not only does this conclusion bear upon the confidence Gentiles can place in their reward for befriending the Jews during the Great Persecution, but it also bears upon our assertion that one of the paths to physical safety during the Great Persecution is following the Jews into the wilderness, where they will be protected by God.

this stressed the need to take the message to the Gentiles, as well. Luke 21:24 lists Gentile nations as the destination of captive Jews from Jerusalem during the Great Persecution and states that Gentiles will trample Jerusalem until the persecution is ended. This leaves only Matthew's sheep and goat judgment in regard to the meaning of τά ἔθνη. Based solely on usage, this term in all probability refers to Gentile nations only in Matthew 25:31–46.

The lack of a prior unambiguous example that our term includes the Israelites favors the conclusion that the Jews are not included in this judgment. When we add the fact that the salvation and restoration of the Jewish nation occurs prior to Armageddon and that the sheep and goat judgment follows Armageddon, this conclusion is certain.

The Timing of National Israel's Salvation

Can we, with certainty, fix the time of Israel's restoration in the sequence of events in connection with the end of the age? The apostle Paul affirms that the salvation of national Israel will occur. He writes in Romans 11:25–26: "For I do not want you, brethren, to be uninformed of this mystery—so that you will not be wise in your own estimation—that a partial hardening has happened to Israel until the fullness of the Gentiles has come in; and so all Israel will be saved."

"Until the fullness of the Gentiles has come in" marks the demarcation of God's work among the Gentiles.[6] During Israel's partial hardening, Gentiles continue to come in. "The fullness" (*to plērōma*) defines how many Gentiles will come. "The fullness" in Louw and Nida means "a total quantity, with emphasis upon completeness—'full number, full measure, fullness, completeness.'"[7] Louw and Nida emphasize the qualitative aspect of *plērōma* – fullness, completeness. However, *plērōma* can also have a quantitative aspect—a full number. Paul seems to refer to "the full number of elect Gentiles that constitutes a representative remnant of the 'Gentile world.'"[8] Thus, Romans 11:25 gives witness to the fact that God's election is numerically absolute.

Dr. Douglas J. Moo concurs. He writes,

> These considerations suggest that the Gentiles' "fullness" involves a numerical completion: God has determined to save a certain number of Gentiles, and only when that number has been reached will Israel's hardening be removed.[9]

The number of Gentiles to be saved is fixed in the mind of God. Paul labels God's election of Gentiles and their subsequent salvation "the mystery of God."[10] This is God's special work among the Gentiles. The salvation and restoration of Israel will follow the completion of this special work. This is confirmed in Acts 15:14–16, which states,

Simeon has related how God first
concerned Himself about taking from
among the Gentiles a people for His name.
With this the words of the Prophets agree,
just as it is written, after these things I will
return, and I will rebuild the tabernacle of
David which has fallen.

How soon after God finishes His work among
the Gentiles He will restore Israel is not indicated.
Yet, Paul argues that Israel's restoration will follow
God's finished business with the Gentile nations.
Thus, we can say with absolute certainty that the
salvation of Israel will not occur before the end of
the Seventieth Week. Daniel 9:24 specifically
demands 490 total years. This conclusively proves
that the salvation of national Israel will not occur
before the end of the final week.

Therefore, we can also argue that *all Israel will
be saved* sometime after "the mystery of God" is
complete. Scholars debate the meaning of "all
Israel will be saved." Dr. Kenneth S. Wuest
argues, "By all Israel being saved, Paul means the
individual salvation of each member of the nation
of Israel living at the time of the Second
Advent."[11] Warren W. Wiersbe states, "All Israel
shall be saved" does not mean that every Jew
who has ever lived will be converted, but that the
Jews living when the Redeemer returns will see
Him, receive Him, and be saved.[12] A.T. Robertson
adds, "The immediate context...argues for the
Jewish people as a whole."[13]

In contradistinction, John A. Witmer writes,

The statement, "All Israel will be saved" does not mean that every Jew living at Christ's return will be regenerated. Many of them will not be saved, as seen by the fact that the judgment of Israel, to follow soon after the Lord's return, will include the removal of Jewish rebels (Ezek. 20:34-38).[14]

However, Witmer fails to understand the timing or nature of God's judgment as reported in Ezekiel 20:34-38. Ezekiel records that the place of judgment for Israel is the "wilderness of the nations." The "wilderness of the nations" is not a geographical location, but as Keil and Delitzsch affirms, is

[a] figurative expression applied to the world of nations, from whom they were indeed spiritually distinct, whilst outwardly they were still in the midst of them, and had to suffer from their oppression. Consequently the leading of Israel out of the nations (v. 34) is not a local and corporeal deliverance out of heathen lands, but a spiritual severance from the heathen world, in order that they might not be absorbed into it or become inseparably blended with the heathen. God will accomplish this by means of severe chastisements, by contending with them as

He formerly contended with their fathers in
the Arabian Desert.[15]

God's promise of restoration must be coupled
with Daniel's prophecy in Daniel 9:24, which
states, "Seventy Weeks have been decreed for
your people and your holy city." Daniel reports
that the Jews and Jerusalem would suffer under a
temporal judgment for 490 years, which mandates
that the spiritual salvation of Israel occur after the
Seventieth Week concludes. So this precludes the
possibility of Israel's salvation before the end of
the Seventieth Week. Therefore, Israel will be
saved after the completion of God's work among
the Gentiles, which coincides with the completion
of the week.

Yet, we must still answer the question, "Does
'all Israel' mean every single Jew alive at that
time?" If this is the case, then it makes no sense to
include them in a sheep and goat judgment. Their
salvation is automatic just after the conclusion of
Daniel's Seventieth Week. *All Israel* means every
single Jew who survives the wrath of Satan and
the trumpet judgments of God's wrath. Two facts
support this conclusion: (1) since a remnant of
Jews experiences salvation presently, only the
salvation of the whole nation is an appropriate
contrast to make sense of the text. If "all Israel"
simply means a few more than a remnant, then
the text makes little sense and offers no real
contrast. (2) According to Romans 26, the
Deliverer will come from Zion with the expressed

purpose of removing ungodliness from Jacob. This same idea follows in Romans 11:27. The heart of the covenant between the Deliverer and Jacob involves taking "away their sins." It makes no sense that if this is the goal of Deliverer's coming, the sins of every Jewish person living at the time will not experience God's forgiveness.

When during the sequence of end-time events *will* the salvation of every single living Jewish person occur? *Kai houtōs* (Καὶ οὕτως) is greatly debated as to its meaning and to the correct translation in Romans 11:26.[16] There are basically two possible nuances of οὕτως (*houtōs*) that fit this context: (1) a model sense, which is reflected in most translations of Scripture and thus the translation "so," "thus," or "in this manner"; and (2) a temporal sense, which is not reflected in any translations of Scripture. This usage would have a possible translation: "then." We agree with Pieter W. van der Horst that a temporal sense is better in this case. He concludes,

> Quite apart from the grammatical and lexical possibilities that the word had, it is also the context in Rom 11 that makes it very probable that it was the temporal meaning of οὕτως that the author had in mind here. His whole argument is based on the idea that it is the precedence of the Gentiles which rouses Israel to jealousy. Only after the Gentiles have fully entered

the covenant, will Israel reenter it, because it first has to be provoked to do so.[17]

Thus, the salvation of all Israel will occur after God completes His special work among the Gentiles, which will coincide with the completion of the Seventieth Week. Also, since the woman of Revelation 12 is only protected for 1,260 days (forty-two months), we believe her salvation must occur immediately because the bowl judgments culminating with Armageddon yet await fulfillment. God protecting the woman from the wrath of Satan and his Antichrist and the first six trumpets but then exposing her to the final wrath of God in bowl judgments does not reflect the sense of Scripture.

Thus, the fact that Paul promises that "all Israel" will be saved after the conclusions of God's work among the Gentiles argues strongly that Jews are not among those judged at the sheep and goat judgment. God's wrath against the Jews ends with the conclusion of Daniel's Seventieth Week, just as He promised in Daniel 9:27.

Zechariah 14: A Confirmation

Since there is a textual basis for our claim that the salvation of national Israel must occur after the Seventieth Week is over, can we in a similar manner show a textual basis for our claim that the judgment and restoration of national Israel occurs prior to the great Armageddon campaign? We believe we can.

Zechariah 14 is helpful at this point. Zechariah 14:1-2 states:

> Behold, a day is coming for the LORD when the spoil taken from you will be divided among you. For I will gather all the nations against Jerusalem to battle, and the city will be captured, the houses plundered, the women ravished, and half of the city exiled, but the rest of the people will not be cut off from the city.

Zechariah begins this chapter by reporting to his audience that Jerusalem's future is bleak. Given the date of Zechariah's prophetic word to Judah and Jerusalem, both the temple and the city were yet to be rebuilt after the destruction by Nebuchadnezzar. Following the modern Western Calendar, scholars typically place the date of Zechariah's writing between 520-518 B.C., according to the Western calendar.

This explains the text's declaration that the temple will be rebuilt (Zech. 1:16). However, at some later date, she will again suffer destruction. This assault will occur before the final restoration and peace to the nation. It is a part of God's cleansing of the nation.

The phrase "a day is coming for the Lord" signals that prophetic fulfillment is in focus here. However, this is not the eschatological

Day of the Lord,[18] which will involve national Israel's deliverance and the destruction of the Gentile nations. It signals that Israel's final years of rebellion and servitude to the nations are imminent.

Before this occurs, God will again allow the people of Jerusalem to be enslaved. Nations of the whole earth will come against Jerusalem and wage war against her. The city will fall and "its houses plundered, and the women raped. Then half of the city will go into exile."

As verse one indicates, after their victory, the winners will divide the spoils of war in the midst of Jerusalem. Zechariah details that this great suffering is God's will. God gathers the nations. His will is not only to purify His people, but to provide an occasion for the destruction of their enemies. Zechariah 14:1–2 describes a fallen city and the subsequent plundering, rape, and deportation.

This unexampled distress (similar to Daniel 12:1), which precedes God's cataclysmic intervention and deliverance, is well known. Dr. Eugene H. Merrill argues,

> Amos is aware of this complex of events when he prophesies of the destruction of all but a remnant of God's people "in that day," followed by the raising up of the fallen tent of David, that is, the revival of the Davidic kingdom (Amos 9:8–15). Joel also knows of a day of destruction (1:15–

2:11) to be followed by divine deliverance (2:18-20; 3:9-21 [HB 4:9-21]). Isaiah, too, predicts the purging of Zion (1:24-31) and her subsequent exaltation among the kingdoms who will, "in the latter days," confess YHWH's sovereignty (2:2-4; cf. 4: 2-6; 26:16 – 27:6; 33:13-24; 59:1 – 60:22; 65:13-25). Micah promises that YHWH will gather the people He has afflicted and that from them He will make the nucleus of a universal kingdom (Mic. 4:6-8). Jeremiah. . . envisions the day when YHWH, having given His people over to destruction and exile, will gather them out of all nations, make a new covenant with them, and bless them with unprecedented prosperity (32:36-44; cf. 33:10-18). Ezekiel adds to this his word of witness when he foresees the purifying wrath of God upon Israel succeeded by their restoration as His servant people in His holy mountain, that is, His kingdom to come. (20:33-44)

It is clear that Zechariah indicates that the capture and mistreatment of the Jews occurs before God's promised salvation. Unexampled distress followed by an eternal deliverance is the template. However, what is not immediately clear is the timing of this event. Was it connected with the destruction of the second temple by Titus? Does it occur prior to the beginning of the second half of

Daniel's final week? Or does it occur during this final period?

In the sequence of end-times events, this sacking of Jerusalem in rather close proximity to the restoration of Judah and Jerusalem is a part of God's discipline of His people prior to their restoration.

Luke 21:20–24 speaks of this event. By using a typological fulfillment pattern, Luke describes an event that will occur twice with very similar outcomes. The first fulfillment is found in the second temple destruction, which is now past. The second fulfillment is yet future. Luke describes it in language very similar to Zechariah 14:2.

One key element helps narrow the time of this yet future fulfillment. Both Zechariah 14:2 and Luke 21:24 indicate that the Jews will be led away as captives "into all the nations." To date, no historical event satisfies the scriptural promise that God "will gather all the nations against Jerusalem to wage war." Neither the second temple destruction nor Armageddon can satisfy this description. Yet, Satan and his Antichrist will come against Jerusalem and fulfill this event as they begin their three-and-a-half years of terror against God's program.

What follows is a description of God's deliverance. It is critical that the reader understand that this event happens before the wrath of God comes against the nations.

Please notice the order of the events:

Then the LORD will go forth and fight against those nations, as when He fights on a day of battle. And in that day His feet will stand on the Mount of Olives, which is in front of Jerusalem on the east; and the Mount of Olives will be split in its middle from east to west by a very large valley, so that half of the mountain will move toward the north and the other half toward the south. And you will flee by the valley of My mountains, for the valley of the mountains will reach to Azel; yes, you will flee just as you fled before the earthquake in the days of Uzziah king of Judah. Then the LORD, my God, will come, and all the holy ones with Him! And it will come about in that day that there will be no light; the luminaries will dwindle. For it will be a unique day which is known to the LORD, neither day nor night, but it will come about that at evening time there will be light. And it will come about in that day that living waters will flow out of Jerusalem, half of them toward the eastern sea and the other half toward the western sea; it will be in summer as well as in winter. (Zech. 14:3-8)

The actual deliverance of Jerusalem and Judea must wait until the completion of Daniel's Seventieth Week. Forty-two months separate Zechariah 12:1-2 and 12:3. Zechariah's allusion to the unexampled distress of God's people is immediately followed by a description of God's deliverance in our text. Yet, there must be a significant amount of time between these two events. The nations take half the Jews back to their homelands. They must also be convinced to return and fight at Armageddon. These and other issues demand a period of time between Zechariah 14:1-2 and 14:3-8.

God's Restoration of All Things

The next major section of Zechariah 14 begins with God, who triumphantly "goes forth" to do battle. Merrill writes,

> This is the language of holy war. . .The Hebrew construction, namely, the use of the infinitive construct of. . ."to fight". . . suggests here a traditional or customary *modus operandi*. . . That is, YHWH will employ the same tactics and strategy and be driven by the same motivations as in the days of old when He entered into conflict with the nations on behalf of His people. The classic example is the defeat of Egypt in the Red Sea at the time of the Exodus, the most graphic account being the poem of celebration of YHWH's triumph, Ex. 15:1-18. . . Zechariah himself has already vividly described YHWH in this role of warrior (9:1-17; 10:4-5; 12:1-9).[19]

Verse 4 of Zechariah 14 returns to the familiar Hebrew expression that signals the eschatological Day of the Lord (בַּיּוֹם־הַהוּא = "in that day"). Thus, one purpose of God's coming is to pour out wrath on His enemies. Zechariah depicts God's arrival in such powerful language that the very topography of the holy land changes. There is no reason to take this in any way other than literally. The effect of His coming spells deliverance for the elect, but trouble for the wicked.

Zechariah describes six steps to God's ultimate deliverance of His people and Jerusalem. First, God's feet will stand on the Mount of Olives. Then, the Mount of Olives will be split from east to west and, finally, the people will flee through the newly created valley.

God comes down and physically stands on the Mount of Olives. Based on New Testament revelation, we know this to be Jesus. This will cause a topographical change. The Mount of Olives will split. Half will move south and half will move north. The "great valley" is described as an escape route for Jerusalem's population. The valley is called by God, "My mountain valley." His people, He says, will flee through it to Azal.

This place is otherwise not mentioned in Scripture, but obviously lies at some distance east of Jerusalem. The need for such means of egress is clear. There will be no time to waste. Indeed, Zechariah compares the urgency of the flight to that which attended the escape from the earthquake in the days of King Uzziah. In a very short time, God will return to Jerusalem for war—thus, the necessity of removing His people so that they do not suffer retaliation at the hands of God's enemy.

After the deliverance of God's people from Jerusalem, three final steps will occur. First, God and His holy ones will come. Then, cosmic lights will be darkened and, finally, living waters will flow from Jerusalem.

It is critical to notice that God comes twice to Jerusalem. First, He comes to deliver His people. Second, He comes to be king over all the earth. This will require war with those who hold the city. God coming to earth with angelic accompaniment for war occurs only at Armageddon. This conclusion has the support of the reference to his "holy ones," which historically and contextually must refer to angels (see Jude 14ff.).

The absence of light leaves no ability to distinguish between day and night. Verse six indicates that all light sources will "congeal." The splendor will make this day unique. Because light sources are lost, only God will know the true day. Light will return at evening. Thus, time is moving contrary to its normal pattern, and Jerusalem will become a source for flowing fresh water. Given the nature of the bowl judgments, which occur between the salvation of Israel and Armageddon, Jerusalem will be the only source of the fresh water on earth.

With God's return, He reclaims temporal lordship over all the earth, which God allowed Satan to exercise since the fall in the Garden. Zechariah 14:9–21 explains:

And the Lord will be king over all the earth. In that day, God will be one and His name one. All the land will be changed into a plain from Geba to Rimmon south of Jerusalem; but Jerusalem will rise and remain on its site from Benjamin's Gate as far as the place of the First Gate to the Corner Gate, and from the Tower of Hananel to the king's wine presses. And people will live in it, and there will be no more curse, for Jerusalem will dwell in security. Now this will be the plague with which the LORD will strike all the peoples who have gone to war against Jerusalem; their flesh will rot while they stand on their feet, and their eyes will rot in their sockets, and their tongue will rot in their mouth. And it will come about in that day that a great panic from the LORD will fall on them; and they will seize one another's hand, and the hand of one will be lifted against the hand of another. And Judah also will fight at Jerusalem; and the wealth of all the surrounding nations will be gathered, gold and silver and garments in great abundance. So also like this plague, will be the plague on the horse, the mule, the camel, the donkey, and all the cattle that will be in those camps. Then it will come about that any who are left of all the nations that went against Jerusalem will go up from year to year to worship the King, the LORD of hosts, and to celebrate the Feast of Booths. And it will be that whichever of the families of the earth does not go up to Jerusalem to worship the King, the LORD of hosts, there will be no rain on them. And if the family of Egypt does not go up or enter, then no rain will fall on them; it will be the plague with which the LORD smites the nations who do not go up to celebrate the Feast of Booths. This will be the punishment of Egypt, and the punishment of all the nations who do not go up to celebrate the Feast of Booths. In that day there will be inscribed on the bells of the horses, "HOLY TO THE LORD." And the cooking pots in the LORD's house will be like the bowls before the altar. And every cooking pot in Jerusalem and in Judah will be holy to the LORD of hosts; and all who sacrifice will come and take of them and boil in them. And there will no longer be a Canaanite in the house of the LORD of hosts in that day.

This cannot be the eternal kingdom, for rebellion against God continues (vv. 13-15) and national distinctions remain between nations (v. 16). Those nations that refuse His sovereignty and fail to do Him obeisance will suffer plague (vv. 17-19). This, too, falls short of an eternal kingdom in which God rules over a redeemed, obedient people. But it is not the kingdom of this age or world either, as the reference to the holiness of all things in it makes clear (vv. 20-21). This can only be the temporal kingdom of God where Jesus rules upon the earth — the kingdom of God.

Zechariah 14:9-21 describes conditions on the earth immediately following God's deliverance of His people and the destruction of the wicked. God's kingship is reestablished. Jerusalem has her families back. All curses are removed against God's people. On the other hand, God will plague the nations. They will literally rot where they stand, leaving their wealth for God's people. Once the battle is over, the peoples under God's rule will make pilgrimages to Jerusalem or suffer God's judgment.

It is critical at this point for the reader to pay close attention to the sequence detailed here. Zechariah 14:12-14 states:

> Now this will be the plague with which the Lord will strike all the peoples who have gone to war against Jerusalem; their flesh will rot while they stand on their feet, and their eyes will rot in their sockets, and their tongue will rot in their mouth. It will come about in that day that a great panic from the Lord will fall on them; and they will seize one another's hand, and the hand of one will be lifted against the hand of another. Judah also will fight at Jerusalem; and the wealth of all the surrounding

nations will be gathered, gold and silver
and garments in great abundance.

The deliverance and restoration of Jerusalem
is an accomplished fact before the judgment
detailed in Zechariah 14:12–14. Judah is fighting
along with the Lord at Jerusalem. A majority of
scholars argue that Zechariah 14:12–15 is a
"parenthetical flashback (the words *the nations
that fought against Jerusalem* look back to v. 2)."[20]
However, this approach fails to appreciate the
sequence presented. When God goes forth to
fight, Jerusalem and her constituents are under
Gentile control. God splits the Mount of Olives
and allows His people to escape to a place of
safety. But in Zechariah 14:12–14, Judah is
fighting in conjunction with God. Therefore, the
restoration of Judah must precede the Lord's
physical return to set up His kingdom. Verses 12–
15 do not constitute a parenthetical flashback, but
rather the correct sequence of events. The
restoration of Israel precedes God's reclamation
of the earth, which includes Armageddon.

This sequence has support in the Revelation to
John. Revelation 11:15–18 states:

Then the seventh angel sounded; and there
were loud voices in heaven, saying, "The
kingdom of the world has become the
kingdom of our Lord and of His Christ; and
He will reign forever and ever." And the
twenty-four elders, who sit on their thrones

before God, fell on their faces and worshiped God, saying, "We give You thanks, O Lord God, the Almighty, who are and who were, because You have taken Your great power and have begun to reign. And the nations were enraged, and Your wrath came, and the time came for the dead to be judged, and the time to reward Your bond-servants the prophets and the saints and those who fear Your name, the small and the great, and to destroy those who destroy the earth."

In close proximity to the sounding of the seventh and final trumpet, which precedes the events connected with Armageddon (Rev. 16:13–16), God Almighty reclaims His physical kingship over the earth. Only after the start of the physical rule of God on earth will the following occur: (1) God's final wrath comes to earth (including Armageddon); (2) God judges the dead; (3) God rewards His bond-servants, the prophets, and the saints; and (4) God destroys those who destroy the earth.

Again, the sequence reveals that the salvation and restoration of God's creation precedes His final wrath against the nations, which will include Armageddon. Revelation 10:7 states, "But in the days of the voice of the seventh angel, when he is about to sound, then the mystery of God is finished, as He preached to His servants the prophets." The "mystery of God," which finishes prior to the sounding of the seventh trumpet, is God's special work among the Gentiles to bring some to glory.[21] Therefore, it is possible for the salvation and restoration of national Israel to occur in close proximity to the actual sounding of the seventh trumpet.

Since the reward of the righteous sheep at the sheep and goat judgment is entrance into the kingdom of God, the battle of Armageddon must have finished prior to the beginning of that judgment — particularly so, given that no fighting follows this judgment. Yet, God exhorts the people of the land of Judah:

> Go, my people! Enter your inner rooms! Close your doors behind you! Hide for a little while, until his angry judgment is over! For look, the Lord is coming out of the place where he lives, to punish the sin of those who live on the earth. The earth will display the bloodshed on it; it will no longer cover up its slain. At that time the Lord will punish with his destructive, great, and powerful sword Leviathan the fast-moving serpent, Leviathan the squirming serpent; he will kill the sea monster. (Isa. 26:20–27:1)

This indicates that Judah's restoration is complete before God finishes His warfare against the wicked. This places the Jews outside the judgment detailed in Matthew 25. Taken together, these facts strongly support our conclusion that Jews are not involved in the judgment of Matthew 25.

Matthew 24:40: A Final Confirmation

One final argument supports our belief that Jews are not involved in the judgment of Matthew 25. In Matthew 25:40, the Lord states that it is the treatment "of these brothers of Mine" by the nations that will determine which members of each nation receive the privilege of physical entrance into God's kingdom. "These brothers of mine" can refer either to the Jews (physical brothers of Jesus) or believers (those born again spiritually). Scholars do not agree concerning the object of the Lord's remarks. They argue for two possible interpretations: (1) some or all of Christ's disciples (the majority view); (2) any needy people in the world (the minority view).[22]

It is our contention that the phrase "these brothers of mine" refers to Jews only. Thus, the sheep and goat judgment is a judgment of all living Gentiles who survive the outpouring of the wrath of God and now must answer for their treatment of the Jews during the final half of Daniel's Seventieth Week. This unique group has two marks of identity: (1) they are called "brothers" and (2) they are the "least."

The Lord Jesus states that individual members of the nations had interaction with His brothers and either were or were not merciful to them when they needed help the most. In Matthew's gospel, the Lord used the term "brother" to refer to racial relations (4:18; 5:47) and to spiritual relations (5:24; 12:50). It is therefore possible that Matthew 24:40 could refer to either type of relationship. Consequently, this term is not conclusive as to its reference in and of itself.[23]

The second mark is more helpful in identifying the Lord's brothers. The Greek literally says, "one of these the brothers of me the least." The NIV suggests, "one of the least of these brothers of mine." The ESV reads, "one of the least of these my brothers." The fact that Matthew 25:45 repeats, "one of the least of these" is helpful in understanding the Lord's intent. The context is clear that "the least of these my brothers" refers to a group of individuals who are either in or shall enter into the temporal kingdom of Christ.

Two Classes in the Kingdom

The kingdom of God will have at least two classes of people, the faithful and the not so faithful.[24] The Lord Jesus repeatedly warns His followers not to be found in a state of unreadiness. In our Lord's parable of the talents, it is painfully clear that faithfulness will be rewarded and unfaithfulness will cause one to suffer. This might include the loss of public recognition, loss of position, or loss of participation in certain kingdom events. It is our belief that one effect of lack of faithfulness will be the classification "least" in the kingdom.

Matthew 5:19 states, "Whoever then annuls one of the least of these commandments, and teaches others to do the same, shall be called least in the kingdom of heaven; but whoever keeps and teaches them, he shall be called great in the kingdom of heaven."

Are the ones who are "called least in the kingdom of heaven" actually in the kingdom of heaven? As it relates to kingdom constituents, those who did not enter God's kingdom are generally labeled "the wicked." Those in the kingdom will have little regard for those who were banished to the eternal fire. Therefore, it is highly unlikely that the phrase "called least in the kingdom of heaven" refers to lost individuals. The term "least" (ἐλάχιστος = *elachistos*) is a Greek superlative and describes that kingdom member who has little to show for his inclusion in God's kingdom.

Some argue that "The metaphorical language of *least* and *great* in the kingdom is reflective of the Matthean interest in rank and degrees of reward in heaven (cf. 11:1; 6:1; 10:41–42; 19:29; 25:21, 23)."[25]

The Lord is signaling real consequences for unfaithfulness. Matthew 19:30 warns that "many who are first will be last, and the last, first." This paradoxical statement is explained by the parable of the household manager who follows in Matthew 20:1–16. The parable illustrates that the amount of time one works does not determine one's pay. Rather, wages are set by the household manager at the time of hire. As the parable illustrates, God's generosity may seem unfair to some, but it is not. This supports our claim. God is generous and willing to grant salvation to all, but He will only grant recognition and commendation to those who are faithful.

This aptly describes many Jews who will be standing with Jesus at the sheep and goat judgment. In light of Paul's statement that "all Israel" will be delivered if they survive the Day of the Lord, it will be clearly recognizable that many will have nothing but the grace of God to thank for it.

Unlike the "greatest in the kingdom" who lived in such a way as to warrant the designation, many of the Jews will have lived so as to warrant the title "least in the kingdom." They are least because they did absolutely nothing. Having been saved just after the end of Daniel's final week, they will not live a single day as faithful followers of Jesus Christ. A significant number will have been saved for less than two months, and as such, they will be unable to walk by faith for any length of time so as to earn the title "greatest in the kingdom."

The Essence of Matthew 25:34–46

With all this in mind, we can look in detail at Matthew 25:34–46:

> Then the King will say to those on His right, 'Come, you who are blessed of My Father, inherit the kingdom prepared for you from the foundation of the world. 'For I

was hungry, and you gave Me something to eat; I was thirsty, and you gave Me something to drink; I was a stranger, and you invited Me in; naked, and you clothed Me; I was sick, and you visited Me; I was in prison, and you came to Me.' Then the righteous will answer Him, 'Lord, when did we see You hungry, and feed You, or thirsty, and give You something to drink? And when did we see You a stranger, and invite You in, or naked, and clothe You? When did we see You sick, or in prison, and come to You?' The King will answer and say to them, 'Truly I say to you, to the extent that you did it to one of these brothers of Mine, even the least of them, you did it to Me.' Then He will also say to those on His left, 'Depart from Me, accursed ones, into the eternal fire which has been prepared for the devil and his angels; for I was hungry, and you gave Me nothing to eat; I was thirsty, and you gave Me nothing to drink; I was a stranger, and you did not invite Me in; naked, and you did not clothe Me; sick, and in prison, and you did not visit Me.' Then they themselves also will answer, 'Lord, when did we see You hungry, or thirsty, or a stranger, or naked, or sick, or in prison, and did not take care of You?' Then He will answer them, 'Truly I say to you, to the extent that you did not do it to one of the least of these, you did not do it to Me.' These will go away into eternal punishment, but the righteous into eternal life.

Jesus separates the sheep from the goats. It is important to remember that whether one is a sheep or a goat is determined long before one stands before the King. Jesus merely identifies what already is. To physically (in an unglorified body) enter the temporal kingdom of God, one must survive the Day of the Lord and be righteous, which includes kindness towards the Jews. He separates the righteous (sheep) from the wicked (goats). The righteous are put on the right-hand side, which is a place of honor and favor. The left is the place of the wicked, the place of dishonor. Please notice that the separation occurs before the pronouncements of the King.

After the division is complete, verse 34 indicates that the King will pronounce judgment. For those on the right, He states, "Come, you who are blessed of My Father, inherit the kingdom prepared for you from the foundation of the world." The elect sheep are bid to come close. "You who are blessed of My Father" indicates that they have a history with God. "You who are blessed" translates the Greek word *eulogeō* (εὐλογέω). It is from this word that we get out English word "eulogy," which literally means "good words." It subsequently came to mean "to bless." It occurs in the perfect tense, which means that this blessing occurs in the long-ago past, but the result continues. In this case, the blessing continues throughout all of eternity. HALLALUJAH!

Evidently, these are blessed in the sense that God the Father has spoken well of them. "Inherit the kingdom prepared for you from the foundation of the world" signals when and how the Father blessed the sheep. "To inherit" speaks of more than mere entrance into God's temporal kingdom. It also speaks of the rights and privileges of the inheritor.

"From the foundation of the world" (ἀπὸ καταβολῆς κόσμου) is a technical phrase used throughout the New Testament to refer to the absolute beginning of creation. Thus, divine election is the basis of the blessing the sheep enjoy. God spoke well of the sheep before they were sheep in that He picked them for His kingdom (Eph. 1:3–12), when they were mere thoughts in the mind of God.

Verse 35 continues with an explanation of the tangible evidence for why God continues to extend favor to the sheep. This issue also supports our claim that the Jews are the focus of the Lord's reference to "the least of these my brothers." It concerns acts of mercy. The days following the evacuation of God's elect to heaven will prove to be extremely trying times on the earth. However, the Lord delineates seven acts of mercy that Gentiles might extend to Jews during this time. Notice that each act will require actions that involve personal sacrifice and possible exposure of oneself to public ridicule and persecution. The seven possible ways to assist are:

- "For I was hungry, and you gave Me something to eat";
- "I was thirsty, and you gave Me something to drink";
- "I was a foreigner, and you took Me in with you";
- "I was naked, and you threw something around Me";
- "I was sick, and you sought and cared for Me";
- "I was in prison, and you came to Me."

When understood in the context of the Great Persecution, it is clear that these life-saving acts will require significant courage on the part of those offering them. It also suggests that these Jews are among the nations and not in the land of Israel. They are perhaps waiting trial or execution. It is imperative to understand that they are not saved during the time they receive kindness from Gentiles.

Scripture speaks in great detail concerning those Jews who live in Jerusalem and Judea during the final half of Daniel's yet future week. On the contrary, few specifics are given to us regarding those not living in Israel. Isaiah 66:18–24 states:

I hate their deeds and thoughts! So I am coming to gather all the nations and ethnic groups; they will come and witness my splendor. I will perform a mighty act among them and then send some of those who remain to the nations—to Tarshish, Pul, Lud (known for its archers), Tubal, Javan, and to the distant coastlands that have not heard about me or seen my splendor. They will tell the nations of my splendor. They will bring back all your countrymen from all the nations as an offering to the Lord. They will bring them on horses, in chariots, in wagons, on mules, and on camels to my holy hill Jerusalem," says the Lord, "just as the Israelites bring offerings to the Lord's temple in ritually pure containers. And I will choose some of them as priests and Levites," says the Lord. "For just as the new heavens and the new earth I am about to make will remain standing before me," says the Lord, "so your descendants and your name will remain. From one month to the next and from one Sabbath to the next, all people will come to worship me," says the Lord. "They will go out and observe the corpses of those who rebelled against me, for the maggots that eat them will not die, and the fire that consumes them will not die out. All people will find the sight abhorrent.

Isaiah 66:18-24 speaks of Armageddon and subsequent events. God will gather the nations and display His glory, which will result in a great host slain by the Lord. Still, God will allow some to escape His wrath. These will act as God's envoys to their own people groups. There, they will report all that they saw and experienced. They will take home to Israel those Jews who survived God's Day-of-the-Lord wrath. In fulfillment of Romans 11:25–26, every Jew who survives will experience the grace and mercy of God. These will come home to Jerusalem via the Gentiles who survived. Their conduct towards the Jews is critical. Those Gentiles who offered kindness to them will experience God's grace.

Matthew 25:41–46 records the outcome of those who refused kindness to suffering Jews. Theirs is eternal punishment. To be sure, their actions toward the Jews are symptomatic of their true heart condition. Their failure to demonstrate compassion is met with God's lack of compassion. If they had demonstrated compassion towards the Jews, perhaps God would have given them grace. Exactly what those grace acts would mean, we cannot say with certainty.

Conclusion

For those who truly know Jesus Christ, physical deliverance away from the Great Persecution will involve the Jews. Follow the Jews who head away from Judea to the mountains/wilderness and receive God's protection until the Lord comes in the air. This is a sure way to survive the persecution of Satan and his Antichrist.

---

[1] Since Daniel 9:27 points out that hostility against God's people is limited to three-and-a-half years, we believe that this and other passages indicate that Satan's wrath will trouble God's people during the second half of this prophetic period.

[2] Naturally, one will need to place his or her faith in the finished work of Jesus Christ. This is how one gains spiritual salvation. However, entering the kingdom of God in a physical body will require faithfulness. Revelation 20:4 speaks of those who died because they were unwilling to compromise by taking the mark or worshiping the beast. These will receive a special resurrection to reign with Christ in the temporal kingdom. Others who are kind towards the Jews will also receive this special privilege. Those who compromise will suffer death.

[3] Marvin Richardson Vincent, *Word Studies in the New Testament*, 1:135 (Bellingham, WA: Logos Research Systems, Inc., 2002).

[4] The word is used of (a) all nations except Israel (Luke 2:32); (b) that part of the Promised Land that was occupied by non-Jews or heavily influenced by them (Matt. 4:15); (c) godless (non-Jewish) people (Matt. 6:32; 10:18; 12:18, 21; 20:25; Luke 12:30); or (d) the Romans (Matt. 20:19; Mark 10:33; Luke 18:32). See Eugene W. Pond, "Who Are the Sheep and Goats in Matthew 25:31–46?" *BSac* 159:635 (July 2002), 295, for a defense of this position.

[5] This is not the gospel of Christ (death, burial, and resurrection for the forgiveness of sin), but the gospel of the kingdom, which announces the imminent outbreak of God's wrath to remove wickedness from the earth. For a detailed discussion of the distinction between the "gospel of Christ" and "the gospel of the Kingdom," see *God's Elect and the Great Tribulation*, Chapter 7.

[6] ἄχρι οὗ [*achri hou*] ("until which time") is a temporal clause and marks the limitations or boundary of the partial hardening.

[7] Louw and Nida, 59:32.

[8] J. Lanier Burns, "The Future of Ethnic Israel in Romans 11," in *Dispensationalism, Israel and the Church*, eds. Craig A. Blaising and Darrell L. Bock (Grand Rapids: Zondervan Publishing House, 1992), 211.

[9] Douglas J. Moo, *The Epistle to the Romans* (Grand Rapids: William B. Eerdmans Publishing Company, 1996), 719. Moo argues

that "the imagery of 'coming in'" fits a numerical concept best. (See Moo, *The Epistle to the Romans*, 718).

[10] Μυστήριον ("mystery") is the better reading in 1 Corinthians 2:1. Thus, Paul refers to "the mystery of God" both here and in Colossians 2:2 and contextually defines it as God's special work among Gentiles to bring some to glory.

[11]Kenneth S. Wuest, *Wuest's Word Studies from the Greek New Testament: For the English Reader*, Rom. 11:26 (Grand Rapids: Eerdmans, 1997, c1984).

[12]Warren W. Wiersbe, *The Bible Exposition Commentary*, "An exposition of the New Testament comprising the entire 'BE' series"—Jkt., Rom. 11:25 (Wheaton, Ill.: Victor Books, 1996, c1989).

[13]A.T. Robertson, *Word Pictures in the New Testament*, vol. V c1932, vol. VI c1933 by Sunday School Board of the Southern Baptist Convention, Ro 11:26 (Oak Harbor: Logos Research Systems, 1997).

[14]John F. Walvoord, Roy B. Zuck, and Dallas Theological Seminary, *The Bible Knowledge Commentary: An Exposition of the Scriptures*, 2:486 (Wheaton, IL: Victor Books, 1983–c1985).

[15]Carl Friedrich Keil and Franz Delitzsch, *Commentary on the Old Testament*, 9:161 (Peabody, MA: Hendrickson, 2002).

[16] Pieter W. van der Horst, "'Only Then Will All Israel Be Saved': A Short Note on The Meaning of καὶ οὕτως in Romans 11:26," *JBL* 119 (2000) 521.

[17] Ibid., 524.

[18] Heb. בַּיּוֹם הַהוּא, (in that day) occurs in Zechariah 9:16; 11:11; 12:3, 4, 6, 8, 9, 11; 13:1, 2, 4; 14:3, 4, 6, 8, 9, 13, 20, 21. Note the particular concentration within the 45 verses of chapters 12–14. However, Zecharaiah 14:1 does not have this typical phrase. Rather, הִנֵּה יוֹם־בָּא לַיהוה ("Look, a day is coming to God") begins Zechariah 14:1. This is not the eschatological Day of the Lord, but begins the process that will eventuate into it and provides a motivation for it to come.

[19] http://www.bible.org/page.php?page_id=511.

[20] The Bible Knowledge Commentary: An Exposition of the Scriptures, 1:1571.

[21] The phrase "mystery of God" occurs two other times in Scripture. It occurs as a textual variant in 1 Corinthians 2:1. The variant

reading is not adopted by the NASB, which takes the reading "testimony." However, the United Bible Society adopts the reading "mystery." Neither significantly changes Paul's meaning. The Corinthians were Gentile believers whom the apostle Paul evangelized during his second missionary journey (Acts 18). In 1 Corinthians 2, Paul defends his message as derived through the Spirit and not the wisdom of man. That message is summarized in the statement, "For I determined to know nothing among you except Jesus Christ, and Him crucified. Contextually, we conclude that "the crucified (1 Cor. 2:2) refers to Jesus Christ. Paul indicates in 1 Corinthians 2:7 that this unique message of which Christ is the center is, in fact, spoken "in a mystery." Based on 1 Corinthians 2, we are able to conclude that the "mystery of God" concerns Jesus Christ and His crucifixion.

The second occurrence is found in Colossians 1:24–2:3. In this passage the apostle Paul writes, "Now I rejoice in my sufferings for your sake, and in my flesh I do my share on behalf of His body, which is the church, in filling up what is lacking in Christ's afflictions. Of *this church* I was made a minister. . . so that I might fully carry out the *preaching* of the word of God, *that is*, the mystery [of God] which has been hidden from the *past* ages and generations, but has now been manifested to His saints, to whom God willed to make known what is the riches of the glory of this mystery [of God] among the Gentiles, which is Christ in you, the hope of glory. We proclaim Him. . . so that we may present every man complete in Christ. . . For I want you to know how great a struggle I have on your behalf. . . that [your] hearts may be encouraged. . . *resulting* in a true knowledge of God's mystery, *that is*, Christ *Himself* in whom are hidden all the treasures of wisdom and knowledge" (emphasis added).

In Colossians 1:26, Paul declares the Word of God, which he preaches, to be a mystery. "This mystery is so rich with glory that God desired to make it known to the saints" (1:27). He states, "The mystery is, *Christ in you* [Gentiles], *the hope of glory*" (emphasis added). Again in Colossians 2:2, he states, "Jesus Christ is the mystery of God." An obvious question concerns whether these two occurrences refer to the same thing. The context indicates that Jesus Christ is the primary focus of the first two chapters of Colossians. His special work among the Gentiles is Paul's primary concern. The particular passage quoted above could be summarized as follows: Paul preaches Christ among the Gentiles because God has a plan to present many Gentiles in glory when Christ returns. Therefore, the mystery of God is God's special work in Christ to bring Gentiles to glory.

Peter states in Acts 15:14–16 that "God first concerned Himself about taking from among the Gentiles a people for His name" and "after these things, I will return and rebuild the tabernacle of David." This passage establishes a very important connection between God's special work in Christ to bring Gentiles to glory and Israel's restoration. Similarly, Romans 11:25–26 states that the mystery of Israel's partial hardening will continue "until the fullness of the Gentiles has come in; and so all Israel will be saved." This passage highlights two facts. First, God has determined a specific number of Gentiles to be saved. Second, the completion of the salvation of the Gentiles will lead to Israel's salvation.

Most scholars recognize the close relationship between the books of Ephesians and Colossians. "Colossians has significant parallels to other Pauline writings. The most extensive parallels occur with Ephesians (Melick: *Philippians, Colossians, Philemon, NAC*, page 171)." It is therefore no surprise that when discussing the same issue in Ephesians, Paul states his insight into the "mystery of Christ," which he defines as "the Gentiles are fellow heirs and fellow members of the promise in Christ Jesus through the gospel" (Eph. 3:4–6).

Returning to Revelation 10, we argue that the "mystery of God" is God's special work in Jesus Christ to bring many Gentiles to glory. This effort on the part of God concludes or is finished just prior to the sounding of the seventh and final trumpet.

[22]Craig Blomberg, Vol. 22, *Matthew*, electronic ed., Logos Library System; *The New American Commentary* (Nashville: Broadman & Holman Publishers, 2001, c1992), 377.

[23] Yet, Matthew demonstrates that the Lord emphasized the spiritual relationship over the physical (12:50; 28:10).

[24] I understand that there are those who believe all of those in the kingdom will be faithful followers of Jesus Christ; otherwise, they lost their salvation. This idea we shall not entertain.

---

[25]Keener, C. S. (1997). *Vol. 1: Matthew*, Matt. 5:19, The IVP New Testament Commentary Series, (Downers Grove, Ill.: InterVarsity Press, 1997).

Chapter 6

Faith: What Is It?

If following the Jews as they flee from Judea to the safety of God's protective custody is not an option, believers will have but one other option for surviving the Great Persecution—faith. The physical survival of the persecution of Satan and his Antichrist is the expressed prerogative of God's sovereign will for His elect. Consequently, how a believer responds to the circumstances of this terrifying period ultimately will come down to faith. Will we trust God or not, even if death or life is the outcome of it all? Will we have "enough" faith to survive this terrible time? These questions demand that we take a detailed look at the whole matter of biblical faith.

Just how important faith is to the Christian life is easily discerned. One biblical writer states, "Now without faith it is impossible to please God, for the one who approaches him must believe that he exists and that he rewards those who seek him" (Heb. 11:6, author's translation). In another place, Scripture says, "The righteous shall live by faith." Yet, most Christians must admit that though this topic is so important to the relationship between God and man, it is very confusing. The most difficult question is, how do we get faith, or grow it once we have it? How precisely, then, does one live by faith, walk by faith, "fight the good fight" of faith, and have access to God by faith?[1]

At first glance, one would think that Hebrews 11:1, which states, "Now faith is being sure of what we hope for, being convinced of what we do not see," at least defines what faith is. After all, it clearly says, "Now faith is. . ." Yet, when defining the term "faith," English dictionaries do not repeat Hebrews 11:1 as a technical definition. In fact, Dictionary.Com defines "faith" as "confidence or trust in a person or thing; belief that is not based on proof; belief in God, doctrines, or teachings of religion; belief in anything; a system of religious belief; the obligation of loyalty or fidelity to a person, promise, or engagement."[2]

This is very similar to the definition one finds in *The Greek–English Dictionary of the New Testament*, which defines the Greek term *pistis* ("faith") as

> *faith, trust, belief; the Christian faith; conviction, good conscience* (Ro 14.22, 23); perhaps *body of faith, doctrine* (Jd 3, 20); *assurance, proof* (Ac 17.31); *promise* (1 Tm 5.12).[3]

A comparison of Hebrews 11:1 and Dictionary.Com reveals a distinction. The website attempts to define *what faith is*, while Hebrews 11:1 seems to illustrate or give an example of *what faith does*. When one looks at terms used in the New Testament—namely, the three Greek words *pistis* (the noun "faith"), *pisteuō* (the verb "to believe"), and *pistos* (the adjective "faithful"), it appears that Dictionary.Com comes closest to defining the meaning of the term "faith."[4]

Faith in the Writings of Paul

Pistis, pisteuō, and *pistos* appear throughout the New Testament as the single most important term for describing how man correctly relates to God. Regarding the writings of the apostle Paul, Martin O. Massinger concludes that these terms have a consistent meaning. He writes,

In its customary meaning of believe, much the same can be said of the verb as was claimed for the noun. Thus it is necessary, in the first place, to point out that to believe means to have a strong conviction about the truthfulness of a proposition. It does not signify merely to suppose or presume, as so often is the case in modern English with the word believe. To believe is the opposite of to doubt. As with the noun, too, to believe is not equivalent to either knowing or being credulous. The element of trust distinguishes believing from both of these lines of action.[5]

He concludes his lengthy discussion of faith by saying that "wherever and however it is exercised, is an attitude of trust in a person, with certain very definite emotional elements."[6]

'Faith' in John's Gospel

In an article entitled, "The Concept of Faith in the Fourth Gospel," Gerald F. Hawthorne writes,

It is significant to observe. . .that although some form of the verb πιστεύειν (*to believe*) is used 98 times, never once does the noun form for faith (πίστις) appear in the gospel of John. . . As would be. . .expected, πιστεύειν with the dative occurs several times. This is the common classical construction and during classical times had two meanings: (1) *trust, believe, put faith in, rely on* a person or thing; and (2) *entrust* something to another. It would appear that the ideas of "believe" and "believe in" were run together in classical times with no care at all being taken to distinguish between these concepts.

He continues,

John uses πιστεύειν with the dative 18 times. Whatever meaning is to be attached to the other constructions used with πιστεύειν it seems pretty clear that πιστεύειν with the dative in John carries with it the idea of "to believe," or "to put confidence in" what someone has to say, "to give credence to," "to accept as true" what one discloses.[7]

Hawthorne concludes,

The favorite Johannine construction, however, is πιστεύειν εἰς followed by the accusative. This expression can be said to be original with the New Testament writers, and an important construction for their message. It is used by them 45 times. . . Thus "believing in" is equated with receiving, and receiving is the opposite of rejecting or refusing.[8]

Faith to John was not static or passive but dynamic and active, reaching out to appropriate and make the object of faith one's own. There was in it, too, an element of dependency, recognition of the absolute need for the object, with a consequent willingness to come to that object. It also appears to be more than mere belief about or recognition of the true value of the object. It appears to be more than mental apprehension of it. There seems to have been a concept of committal to that object—one step beyond perception.[9]

H. Phillip Hook would add,

> In attempting to define faith it would be well to start by analyzing the elements that compose such a faith. There seem to be at least three of these elements clearly set forth in Scripture. The first of these is knowledge and assent to that knowledge. A second element is trust or dependence which appropriates the knowledge to one's self. The final element is the product of faith, thus demonstrating its reality. These three in proper relationship are of considerable value in understanding the whole.[10]

James I. Packer stipulates,

> [T]he central core of the biblical concept of faith, that which is distinctive and characteristic of faith in the New Testament

is precisely that it is *faith*. Faith is a matter of believing (πιστεύω) εἰς (into) or ἐπί (down upon) Jesus Christ, the living Lord.[11] Finally, one other adds,

> *Pistis*, the common Greek word for faith, can be passive or active, on the one hand meaning "fidelity," or "trustworthiness," and on the other "faith," or "trust." In the overwhelming majority of cases faith, as the New Testament rendering of *pistis*, means "reliance," or "trust." However, each individual occurrence [sic] of this term requires close examination to insure [sic] the correct intent of the author. *Pistis* as used in Luke 8:25 clearly means "faith" — the kind of faith that leads to salvation. On the other hand, Romans 3:3 clearly does not mean faith that leads to salvation. Rather, a component of God's character is in view. Faithfulness is a much better translation of *pistis* here.[12]

As one can see, there are slight nuances to the meaning of faith reflected in the views of the authors quoted above. However, what seems to be true is this: The objects of faith are propositional facts. Thus, ultimately one does not believe in Jesus as an object in order to be saved. Rather, one believes propositional facts stated about Jesus. One believes that Jesus is the Son of God. One believes that Jesus died for his or her sins. One believes that Jesus rose from the dead. One believes that Jesus is God. One believes that Jesus saves sinners from their sin. All of these are statements of fact.

Regarding faith and the propositions stated above, we ask a very important question: Is it possible to believe only to a *certain degree* regarding these truths? If so, then to what degree must one believe for his or her faith to be authentic? Is ten percent sufficient? Or must one believe at least fifty-one percent? Does the idea of growing in faith suggest that one is able to incrementally increase the size of one's faith in or towards something or someone? Let's examine the New Testament regarding this matter.

On two occasions, the apostle Paul uses the verb "to grow" in connection with faith. In 2 Corinthians 10:15, Paul writes, "Nor do we boast beyond certain limits in the work done by others, but we hope that as your faith continues to grow, our work may be greatly expanded among you according to our limits."In a similar sense, he also writes in 2 Thessalonians 1:3, "We ought to thank God always for you, brothers and sisters, and rightly so because your faith flourishes more and more."

Commenting on the meaning of 2 Thessalonians 1:3, one author writes,

> A parallel understanding of faith as something that increases and leads to greater commitment to the beliefs and

practices of the Christian religion occurs in 2 Cor. 10:15 where the simple form of αὐξάνειν ("to increase") is found. This is a very different understanding of faith from the dominant one in the later Pastoral Epistles. In the Pastorals faith is frequently viewed as a fixed set of beliefs to which Christians must adhere (cf. 1 Tim. 2:19; 5:8; 2 Tim. 1:5). On the basis of 1 Thess. 1:3, we can be certain that Paul had in mind an increase of faith manifesting itself in the deeds of the Thessalonians and especially in the way they had withstood opposition and persecution, as 2 Thess. 1:4 demonstrates.[13]

If one takes Scripture at face value, then it would seem that Paul does teach that one can incrementally increase the size of his or her faith. Or does he?

A form of the Greek verb *auxanō* (αὐξάνω) occurs in both passages just quoted. It does have the basic meaning "cause to increase, cause to grow." It is therefore the context of each passage that must answer the question of what is growing or increasing. In 2 Corinthians 10:15, Paul expresses hope that as the faith of the Corinthians goes on increasing, he will have success in spreading the gospel to more and more people.

Therefore, how does the ongoing increase of faith on the part of the Corinthians contribute to Paul's ability to spread the Gospel? Most commentators see the assistance of Paul by the Corinthians in terms of their prayers, provisions, and push of Paul westward with the message of salvation by grace through Jesus Christ as the expression of the Corinthians' faith. Thus Louw and Nida representatively conclude that "It seems wiser to give πίστις its predominant Pauline meaning of a confident trust in Christ or God that is expressed in good works (Gal. 5:6; 1 Thess. 1:3)."[14] These authors additionally would add that "with an expression of state such as πίστις, intensity of degree seems to be more appropriate.[15]

Thus, it is the opinion of most scholars that Paul believes and teaches that faith grows incrementally in the sense of one's confidence in God and is evidenced in a person's works. However, this seems unlikely, and particularly so, given that Paul addresses the whole church at Corinth as the text demonstrates. He writes, "We hope that as your [plural] faith [singular] continues to grow." That Paul addresses the church as a collective whole argues against the notion that an incremental increase of faith is intended.

In no sense would each individual in the church have the same amount or size of faith regarding a particular matter. In no sense were all the members equal in their confidence about God. How would Paul know this? Only God could know with certainty the percentile of faith held by each individual in the church. Paul could only speak of the necessity for growth in faith to the whole church as a single collective if he is speaking of their faithfulness.

It is possible to speak of the faithfulness of a local church relative to a particular issue. For example, a local church can be faithful in its giving to support a missionary in Africa. However, this does not mean that each and every individual member of that church gives to missions. In fact, we know this is rarely the case.

Murray J. Harris knows of this view but rejects it. He writes, "It is not impossible that πίστις here refers to the Corinthians' 'faithfulness'. . . to his mission assignment."[16] It would appear that the admission of Wayne McDill (of Southeastern Baptist Theological Seminary) that each individual occurrence of the term *pistis* requires close examination to ensure that the correct intent of the author is reflected in the English translation is correct. It is the Corinthians' faithfulness that Paul hopes will increase. Their faithfulness to the cause of spreading the message of the death, burial, and resurrection of Jesus Christ will greatly aid Paul in his efforts.

In a similar fashion, 2 Thessalonians 1:3 speaks of the faithfulness of the Thessalonians. Paul boasts about the Thessalonians' "perseverance and faith in all the persecutions and afflictions" they endured. Again, Paul speaks of the faith (singular) of the church at Thessalonica. Paul could not have known the precise degree of faith held by each individual there. Neither could he have known whether every single individual was growing.

However, all believers are continually in need of growth in terms of their faithfulness to God. The Thessalonians proved their growth in faithfulness in light of their perseverance and faith in all the persecutions and afflictions they endured.

Yet, no details are given concerning those (if any) who abandoned the church because of persecution. However, Paul does indicate that some members of the church in Thessalonica were not walking in personal faithfulness to God. In 2 Thessalonians 3:11, Paul writes, "For we hear that some among you are living an undisciplined life, not doing their own work but meddling in the work of others." This clearly indicates that not all the Thessalonians were faithful in their personal walks before God. Yet, Paul could speak of the whole church as faithful to the Lord with respect to spreading the good news of Jesus Christ.

Therefore, we continue to maintain that faith does not increase incrementally; it does not have degrees. We shall drive home this point in the next chapter.

---

[1]Dallas Theological Seminary, *Bibliotheca Sacra Vol. 109*, 109:263 (Dallas Theological Seminary, 1952; 2002).

[2] http://dictionary.reference.com/browse/faith

[3]Barclay Moon Newman, *Concise Greek–English Dictionary of the New Testament* (Stuttgart, Germany: Deutsche Bibelgesellschaft; United Bible Societies, 1993), 143.

[4]The negatives *apisteuō* (to "not believe") and *apistia/apistos* ("unbelief") are only important in that they help us better understand the meaning of the primary terms *pistis*, *pisteuō*, and *pistos*.

[5]"Paul's Use of the Word Faith Part 1," Martin O. Massinger, *Bibliotheca Sacra Vol. 107*, 107:193 (Dallas Theological Seminary, 1950; 2002).

[6] Bibliotheca Sacra Vol. 109, 109:258 (1952; 2002).

[7] Bibliotheca Sacra Vol. 116, 116:118 (1959; 2002).

[8] *Bibliotheca Sacra Vol. 116*, 116:119-120 (1959; 2002).

[9] Bibliotheca Sacra Vol. 116, 116:122 (1959; 2002).

[10] Bibliotheca Sacra Vol. 121, 121:135 (1964; 2002).

[11] Bibliotheca Sacra Vol. 129, 129:297 (1972; 2002).

[12]Southeastern Baptist Theological Seminary, *Faith and Mission Vol. 12*, vnp.12.1.82 (Southeastern Baptist Theological Seminary, 1995; 2005).

[13]Charles A. Wanamaker, *The Epistles to the Thessalonians: A Commentary on the Greek Text* (Grand Rapids, Mich.: W.B. Eerdmans, 1990), 217.

[14]Murray J. Harris, *The Second Epistle to the Corinthians: A Commentary on the Greek Text* (Grand Rapids, Mich.; Milton Keynes, UK: W.B. Eerdmans Pub. Co.; Paternoster Press, 2005), 720.

[15] Louw and Nida, 1:684.

[16] Harris, *The Second Epistle to the Corinthians: A Commentary on the Greek Text*, 720.

Chapter 7

Faith: Does It Have Degrees?

As stated earlier, faith is the persuasion or conviction that something is true. It causes a person to act or not to act in certain ways in light of a conviction about something. In Acts 17:4, Luke relates concerning the Jews at the synagogue in Thessalonica, "Some of them *were persuaded*." A few verses later, he reports on the response of the Jews at the synagogue in Berea. "Therefore many of them *believed*" (v. 12). Clearly, *the persuasion* of verse 4 is synonymous with *the belief* of verse 12.[1] The people in Thessalonica were persuaded that Jesus is the Messiah who guarantees everlasting life to all who believe in Him.

Was it possible for some of the Thessalonians to believe or be persuaded or convinced, not wholly, but only somewhat? Notice the diagram below:

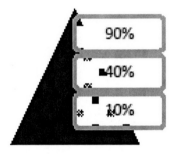

Was it possible for some of the Thessalonians to believe or be persuaded forty, sixty, or ninety percent about the Messiahship of Jesus Christ? If so, this naturally demands that we also answer the question regarding what percentage of faith is necessary to achieve success in any one area. Is it possible to quantify faith in this manner? Again, many would say that the Bible teaches that one can grow in faith. By that they mean that there can be varying degrees of confidence in a given fact or proposition. Thus, we have the popular teachings that one needs to grow in his or her faith.

Dr. Merrill C. Tenney wrote a series of articles on faith in the Gospel of John. He concludes from his study that faith does grow. He writes,

Since belief is connected with action, it involves also progress. The various instances which John has selected to illustrate the rise and growth of belief indicate the stages by which it develops in the normal relationship between an individual and Jesus.[2]

In defense of his conclusion that the Gospel of John depicts the disciples of our Lord progressing in their belief over time, Tenney goes on to write,

This progressive experience is woven into the literary structure of the Gospel, which to some degree combines chronological sequence of events with the disciples' increasing advance in faith. As they traveled and worked with Jesus, observing His methods and listening to His words, the tide of belief rose higher continually. Although it was subject to some ebb and flow, it still persisted until it eventuated in their total commitment to Him and in His parting commission to them.[3]

There is little debate that progressive development in Jesus' disciples is depicted throughout the Gospel of John. Yet, we cannot simply accept at face value that faith in terms of its size is increasing. Therefore, we must look at what way or in what sense the disciples are growing?

We do not agree with Tenney that the disciples are growing in faith, if by faith Tenney means the incremental increase of conviction or persuasion about a single truth. Rather, we see the disciples growing in their knowledge of Jesus Christ, which causes them to respond to what they know by expressing faith in Jesus regarding a particular issue. It becomes very clear that the disciples believed various things about Jesus long before they believed that He is the Son of God sent to save mankind from its sins, an event that would require His death and resurrection.

The first remark about the belief of one of the Lord's disciples occurs in John 1:50. After the Lord summoned Philip of Bethsaida to follow Him, we are told that Philip found Nathanael and informed him, "We have found the one Moses wrote about in the law, and the prophets also wrote about—Jesus of Nazareth, the son of Joseph." Nathanael's response, "Can anything good come out of Nazareth?" reveals his doubts about what Philip said. This doubt will not be easily or quickly dispelled as we shall see throughout the rest of John's gospel.

John then reports,

Jesus saw Nathanael coming toward him and exclaimed, "Look, a true Israelite *in*

whom there is no deceit!" Nathanael asked
him, "How do you know me?" Jesus
replied, "Before Philip called you, when
you were under the fig tree, I saw you."
Nathanael answered him, "Rabbi, you are
the Son of God; you are the king of Israel!"
Jesus said to him, "Because I told you that
I saw you under the fig tree, do you
believe? You will see greater things than
these." He continued, "I tell all of you the
solemn truth—you will see heaven opened
and the angels of God ascending and
descending on the Son of Man." (John
1:47–51, emphasis added)

We know that Nathanael had doubts about the
identity of Jesus prior to meeting Him, having only
heard second-hand information from Philip.
Evidently, the Lord's statement that He saw
Nathanael under a fig tree just prior to Philip's
request that he come and meet the Lord caused a
change in Nathanael's attitude.

Nathanael expresses his sudden conviction
about Jesus with the expression, "Rabbi, you are
the Son of God; you are the king of Israel!"
Unfortunately, most readers see Nathanael's
response and quickly conclude that by the titles
"Son of God" and "king of Israel," he means what
we have come to understand these terms to mean.
Such thinking runs into error.

The fact that Nathanael called the Lord "rabbi," the fact that he employs the titles "Son of God" and "king of Israel," and the fact that the Lord questioned his belief, all support our conclusion that Nathanael's response is one-dimensional. That is, he does not yet understand what the titles really mean when applied to our Lord. Nathanael believes in one facet of a beautifully cut diamond. Since Jesus can see what a man is doing at any given time, Nathanael believes that Jesus is special, but he does not yet understand just how special or why!

The next expression of belief on the part of our Lord's growing band of followers occurs in connection with His miracle of turning water into wine. In reference to this event at a wedding in Cana of Galilee, the Bible states, "Jesus did this as the first of his miraculous signs. . . In this way he revealed his glory, and his disciples believed in him" (John 2:11). If readers conclude from John's statement that the disciples believed that Jesus was the Son of God sent into the world to die on a cross and be raised three days later, they are greatly mistaken. The disciples are on a journey of discovery. Each event in John's gospel reveals a new "facet," or newly acquired information about our Lord. This should have helped them discern the significance of what they were learning and draw the correct conclusions, thereby expanding the basis of their faith. But as we will see, that understanding was slow to come.

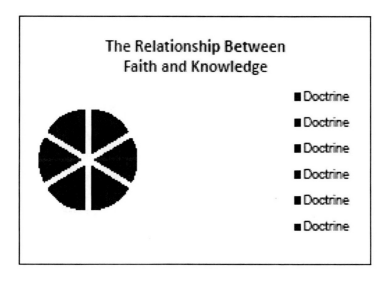

Notice the diagram above. It illustrates the fundamental nature between faith and knowledge. Let's understand this relationship the same way we understand the relationship between a pie and the container in which the pie is baked. The container that holds the pie and gives it shape is faith. Knowledge is the content of the pie. Each slice is an individual truth or conviction. The container does not grow or get any larger; it remains the same. The number of pieces of pie simply changes relative to what one believes about a given issue. The Bible describes the number of "slices" a particular person has regarding any particular issue as that of "unbelief," "little faith," or "great faith." (This matter we shall discuss at great length shortly.)

It is incorrect to describe John's presentation of the disciples' journey as one of growing in faith. The disciples are growing in their knowledge of the Lord, which will allow them to express intelligent faith in the Lord at a given time in relation to a particular circumstance. For example, the disciples will soon be confronted with the need to feed five to six thousand people.

Concerning this need, the Lord asked Philip, "Where can we buy bread so that these people may eat?" It is very informative that the Lord asked Philip this question. John, with a parenthetical remark, informs his readers that Jesus asked the question "to test him." The Greek word that is translated "to test" "corresponds to a large extent to that of English *test* and *try*... [in essence to] *put to some sort of test.*"[4] The purpose or goal of the Lord's test of Philip is clearly in light of his plan to show the disciples what can and should be done.

Earlier, Philip had excitedly told his brother, "We have found the one Moses wrote about in the law, and the prophets also wrote about—Jesus of Nazareth, the son of Joseph" (John 1:45). As we are best able to determine, the sixth chapter of the Gospel of John occurs about one year before the death of our Lord Jesus. Thus, after two-plus years, we have an opportunity to see what Philip has learned. If faith increases in size in the traditional sense, then surely after two plus years, Philip has grown in faith. What he believes should now evidence itself by what he does in response to the Lord's question. Unfortunately, he details the economic reality of the situation, which ultimately speaks to its impossibility from a human perspective.

The graphic below sadly depicts Philips lack of growth in the necessary knowledge to answer the Lord's question. He was ill-prepared to boldly declare his convictions regarding the Lord's abilities in this situation.

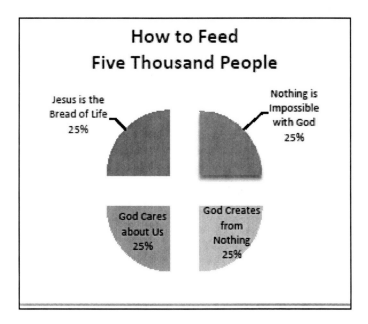

In order for Philip to have received God's commendation as having "great faith," he would have had to have conviction concerning four truths detailed in the chart above. He only needed to have said, "Lord, I do not know, but I know that God can do the impossible. He can create something out of nothing. You are the Bread of Life and love this people. Whatever you tell me to do, I will." By such a response, Philip would have received a commendation from our Lord. In this case, Philip's pie of knowledge would have consisted of four specific doctrines or convictions.

After the miracle at the wedding in Cana, we are not told explicitly what the disciples believed.[5] But we discern from the context that they came to believe or trust Jesus to be a special teacher of God, for John 2:11 reports that in turning water into wine, "He [Jesus] revealed his glory." "Glory" usually refers to a special manifestation of God's presence. Through this sign, Jesus revealed His glory — that He is a special agent of God. This is what the disciples trusted or believed about Him.

The chart below reflects all that the disciples believed about Jesus at this point and is that which constitutes a "little faith." There was very little content to their faith. They believed Jesus to be the "messiah," but they had very little knowledge of what it really meant. Only by adding truths to their knowledge base with the pie be sliced. Until then it remains whole which represents one truth.

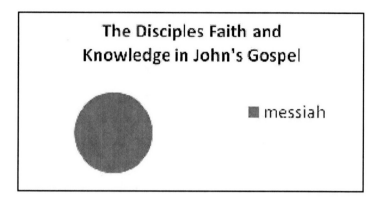

The next explicit reference to the belief of the disciples occurs in John 6:68–69. It is necessary to read the complete story to appreciate the exchange between the disciples and our Lord. John writes,

> I am the bread of life. Your ancestors ate the manna in the wilderness, and they died. This is the bread that has come down from heaven, so that a person may eat from it and not die. I am the living bread that came down from heaven. If anyone eats from this bread he will live forever. The bread that I will give for the life of the world is my flesh."
>
> Then the Jews who were hostile to Jesus began to argue with one another, "How can this man give us his flesh to eat?" Jesus said to

them, "I tell you the solemn truth, unless you eat the flesh of the Son of Man and drink his blood, you have no life in yourselves. The one who eats my flesh and drinks my blood has eternal life, and I will raise him up on the last day…Just as the living Father sent me, and I live because of the Father, so the one who consumes me will live because of me. This is the bread that came down from heaven; it is not like the bread your ancestors ate, but then later died. The one who eats this bread will live forever."

Jesus said these things while he was teaching in the synagogue in Capernaum. Then many of his disciples, when they heard these things, said, "This is a difficult saying! Who can understand it?" When Jesus was aware that his disciples were complaining about this, he said to them, "Does this cause you to be offended? Then what if you see the Son of Man ascending where he was before? The Spirit is the one who gives life; human nature is of no help! The words that I have spoken to you are spirit and are life. But there are some of you who do not believe." (For Jesus had already known from the beginning who those were who did not believe, and who it was who would betray him.) So Jesus added,

"Because of this I told you that no one can come to me unless the Father has allowed him to come."

After this many of his disciples quit following him and did not accompany him any longer. So Jesus said to the twelve, "You don't want to go away too, do you?" Simon Peter answered him, "Lord, to whom would we go? You have the words of eternal life. We have come to believe and to know that you are the Holy One of God!" Jesus replied, "Didn't I choose you, the twelve, and yet one of you is the devil?"

It appears that Jesus intentionally presented facts about Himself in such a way as to drive away those who were following Him with wrong motives. The text indicates that "after this [the Lord's call for His audience to eat his body and drink his blood] many of his disciples quit following him and did not accompany him any longer" (John 6:66). After this, Lord questioned the Twelve about their intentions. In John 6:58-69, Peter answered, "Lord, to whom would we go? You have the words of eternal life. We have come to believe and to know that you are the Holy One of God!"

The Lord readily contradicted Peter's basic assertion. Clearly, not all the disciples believed as Peter declared. John tells us that our Lord corrected Peter regarding Judas, who later proved the Lord's words to be true. Thus, not all the disciples had come to believe and know Jesus as the Holy One of God, which will prove evident at his trial.

In the same way, Peter's words do not convey a profound understanding of God's full intent concerning the Lord's mission. The phrase "the Holy One of God" has a variety of textual variants. Scholars are not sure of exactly what Peter said on this occasion. On various occasions throughout the gospels, we have reports of Peter making confessions about Jesus. In Matthew 16:16, Peter states, "You are the Christ, the Son of the living God." In Mark 8:29, he remarks, "You are the Christ." Finally, in Luke 9:20, he identifies Jesus as "the Christ of God." On each occasion, we hear Peter using terms that he does not fully understand. This is explicit in Mark 8:29. Immediately after declaring to Jesus, "You are the Christ," Peter rebukes the Lord for declaring that He must die (Mark 8:32). The Lord attributes this idea to Satan. Peter clearly did not know what kind of messiah the Lord was. This suggests he did not fully understand Jesus' messiahship or what it truly meant for Him to have come down from heaven as the Son of God.

That Peter declared in John 6:69 that he and the other disciples believed and had come to know our Lord's identity is very helpful. Peter recognized that there was a relationship between belief and knowledge. Obviously, the disciples were growing in their knowledge about Jesus. With this knowledge, they were beginning to express faith in the Lord concerning certain matters. At this point, for the most part, the disciples believed that Jesus might have something to do with the restoration of national Israel in regard to its eschatological hopes (i.e., the land, a Davidic king, and peace and prosperity). We see this in John 6:15, which states, "Then Jesus, because he knew they [the people] were going to come and seize him by force to make him king, withdrew."

This point of view was not limited to the crowd. Therefore, the chart below reflects a growing understanding by the disciples of who Jesus is. Peter is very truthful in John 6:68–69. Some or most of the disciples believed that Jesus was a unique, special person sent from God. In this section, we will continue to use the term "messiah" with a little "m" because they had no idea what that term really meant. Thus, the chart below reflects that the disciples had only one truth to work with. Their pie is undifferentiated. Consequently, the disciples were limited in their ability to express faith in Jesus. They had faith concerning Jesus and their future temporal kingdom on earth. Just how Jesus was going to bring the kingdom about was still very unclear.

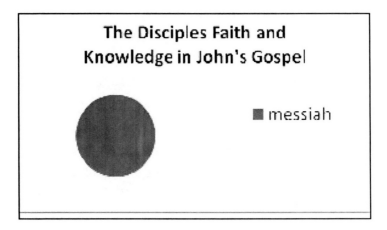

The strongest evidence that the disciples were growing in their knowledge of Jesus, which expressed itself in statements about their faith, occurs in John 11. The incident of Lazarus' death is important for what it teaches us about the disciples' knowledge. According to John 11:8, the disciples understood that the Lord's life was in danger if He went back to Judea. At this point, an attempt already had been made by Jewish leaders in Judea to kill Jesus by stoning.

Our Lord's announcement that He was going back to Judea to awaken Lazarus brought the following response from the disciple Thomas: "Let us go too, so that we may die with him." This is a clear indication that while the disciples believed certain things about Jesus, there were many things they did not yet understand. However, the Lord Jesus states in John 11:14-15, "Lazarus has died, and I am glad for your sake that I was not there, so that you may believe." What is it that He wants the disciples to believe? He is clearly talking to all of them. Yet, John 2:11 indicates that the disciples already "believed in Him." Our Lord is testing the disciples regarding the width and depth of their knowledge, which serves as the basis of faith.

It is our Lord's hope to add to His disciples' knowledge base by showing them the power of God as it relates to death. They are worrying about the death of the Lord and themselves. At this time, they believe that all their hopes and aspirations depend on Jesus remaining alive. If He dies, the disciples feel that they might as well die with Him. However, Jesus will teach them that death is not a hindrance to God's plans. It is just one way God's glory and power manifests itself in this world.

While the Lord called upon Martha to believe in His power to raise the dead (John 11:25), there is no indication that the disciples believed His power to do so. As John rehearses what happened many years after the fact, he does not state the attitudes or convictions of the disciples during the actual event itself. Since we do not have confirmation that they developed this conviction at this point, we will not add it to their knowledge base, which forms the content of their faith.

John 13:19 reports that Jesus told the disciples the night before His death on the cross, "I am telling you this now, before it happens, so that when it happens you may believe that I am he." No one disagrees that the events of John 13 occurred the night before Jesus was to be put to death. But few discern the significance of the fact that He was still calling upon the original Twelve to "believe that I am he" within mere hours of His death.

More importantly, Jesus wanted the foreknowledge of His betrayal to confirm in the minds and hearts of His disciples "that he was, in fact, none other than the *egō eimi* ('I am'), which was the name of the sending God of Exodus 3:14 and the self-designation Jesus used many times in John."[6] At this moment in time, the disciples clearly had still not come to faith in Jesus Christ as God's Son sent to die for their sins. This has more support in John 14:1, where our Lord commands, "Let not your heart be distressed. You believe in God; believe also in me."

It is not doubted that the disciples believed in God, but there is great question about their belief in Jesus at this point. Thus, most scholars understand the verse to mean that Jesus is requesting that His disciples believe in Him to the same degree that they believed in the God of the Old Testament. It should not escape attention that Jesus made this request the very night of the betrayal that would lead to His death the following day.

We know that the disciples believed certain things about Jesus at this point. Yet, Jesus is commanding that they believe in Him regarding His efforts on their behalf to secure a place in God's mansion for them—a feat that requires His departure and return at a later date.

It is within hours of Jesus' trial and death that the eleven declared: "Now we know that you know everything and do not need anyone to ask you anything. Because of this we believe that you have come from God" (John 16:30). As is so typical, the disciples speak out of their ignorance. They assume that they finally understand all that

Jesus has been talking about. On this basis, they declare that Jesus came from God. However, they do not say that they believe He *is* God.

Jesus corrects their impulsive declaration with the truth. They will desert him within hours. They believe He came from God, but the full implications of this fact remain unclear to them. John himself declares in 20:9 that "they [the eleven] did not yet understand the Scripture that Jesus must rise from the dead." Again, their knowledge was inadequate, and that produces a "little faith." Thomas declares prior to the Lord proving His resurrection, "Unless I shall see, I will not believe [that Jesus is alive]" (20:25). It is not difficult to prove that most of the disciples did not have saving faith until after the resurrection. Until then, they were on a journey of discovery.

As we apply the lessons of these events to us today, we must realize that the ability to face the unparalleled persecution of Satan and his Antichrist without compromise likewise will require faith. How will one acquire this faith? Will believers have time to "grow" their faith? Will it be possible to have a "little faith," but not enough to survive this terrible time? To answer these questions, we must first correctly understand the Scriptures.

'Increase Our Faith'

There is one passage in the New Testament that actually uses the term "increase" with respect to faith. It follows the Lord's troubling call for His disciples to live up to a standard beyond their mental comfort zones.

Luke 17:1-4 reports,

> Jesus said to his disciples, "Stumbling blocks are sure to come, but woe to the one through whom they come! It would be better for him to have a millstone tied around his neck and be thrown into the sea than for him to cause one of these little ones to sin. Watch yourselves! If your brother sins, rebuke him. If he repents, forgive him. Even if he sins against you seven times in a day, and seven times returns to you saying, 'I repent,' you must forgive him." (Luke 17:1–4)

The seventeenth chapter of the Gospel of Luke begins, among other things, with a command concerning forgiveness. The Lord instructs His followers to forgive those who sin against them seven times in one day but each time return and ask for forgiveness. Humanly speaking, it would be difficult for anyone to exercise this degree of patience and forgiveness, particularly if the sins are egregious. On its face, such actions would require a true commitment to honor God, regardless of the seeming contradictions to human nature.

After our Lord's startling request, notice what follows in Luke 17:5–10:

> The apostles said to the Lord, "Increase our faith!" So the Lord replied, "If you had faith the size of a mustard seed, you could say to this black mulberry tree, 'Be pulled out by the roots and planted in the sea,' and it would obey you. "Would any one of you say to your slave who comes in from the field after plowing or shepherding sheep, 'Come at once and sit down for a meal'? Won't the master instead say to him, 'Get my dinner ready, and make yourself ready to serve me while I eat and drink. Then you may eat and drink'? He won't thank the slave because he did what he was told, will he? So you too, when you have done everything you were commanded to do, should say, 'We are slaves undeserving of special praise; we have only done what was our duty.'"

Thus, in ordering the material in his gospel, Luke makes an interesting choice. First, he records Jesus' hard saying in 17:1–4. Then, he follows this with the teaching about the servant and his master in 17:5-10, followed by a request on the part of the apostles. He records, "The apostles said to the Lord, 'Increase our faith!'" This request immediately exposes a problem for the reader. What is the connection between Luke 17:1-4 and Luke 17:5-10? Is the flow this chapter a product of Luke's own construction or are the segments in chronological order as the Lord spoke them? Since there are no parallel accounts in the other gospels, we must conclude that Luke has joined these events together to make his own point. Since the primary antagonists in Luke are the Pharisees, at every turn Luke takes the opportunity to show how far off the mark their ways are to what God demands. This the disciples recognized in their own actions.

One author has reasoned that

> "[I]ncrease our faith" could be a direct response to Luke 17:1-4, where Jesus told the disciples to repeatedly forgive those who sin against them and repent. If so, the disciples may be asking something like, "Lord, please help us to believe You about this." It may have been hard for them to believe that acting in this way is a good idea. In that case they would doubt the

wisdom of what He said. Or possibly they doubted not the wisdom of it, but their ability to do what He says. "Increase our faith" would thus be a cry for Jesus to change their thinking so that they see themselves as capable of doing this.

If "Increase our faith" is taken as an indirect response to Luke 17:1-4, then they are saying something like, "Lord, this is revolutionary teaching. We believe that what You are saying is what God wants us to do. Teach us more so that we can know and believe and do the will of the Father in even more areas of our lives." In that case, the apostles here weren't asking for a greater degree of faith in some single proposition. They were asking Jesus to expand their belief system so that His teaching in Luke 17:1-4 naturally fit their worldview.[7]

While this view is possible, the context of what follows makes the nature of their request clear. They were not looking for more information so they could obey God in all matters as suggested above. The first sense comes closer to their intent. The disciples' request is for more faith to do the will of God when it is hard to do (humanly speaking). By the Lord's answer, we see that there were two problems inherent in this request: a misunderstanding about the nature of faith and a misunderstanding about the disciples' responsibility as slaves of God.

The Exegetical Dictionary of the New Testament stipulates that, of the range of possible meanings for the Greek word *prostithēmi* in the New Testament, "The basic meaning "add to" predominates."[8] Thus, the question of the disciples does involve the idea of incremental increase. It is critical that the reader pay very close attention to our Lord's response.

The idea or belief that faith cannot and need not be increased in increments has support in the Lord's reply. He states, "If you had faith the size of a mustard seed, you could say to this black mulberry tree, 'Be pulled out by the roots and planted in the sea,' and it would obey you" (Luke 17:6). The immediate implication of our Lord's comments is obvious. In essence, He tells the disciples that they do not have a faith issue.

The Lord's answer reveals a critically important implication concerning the nature of faith. Given the size of a mustard seed, the size of faith is clearly not the issue. If such a tiny amount of faith could move a large tree in such a dramatic way, *then the issue is never a matter of the size of one's faith, but whether one has faith at all.* In fact, this passage proves that the size of faith is never the issue. One either has faith or he does not.

It is critical that the reader pay very close attention here. Surviving the persecution of Satan and his Antichrist will not require a huge amount of faith. In fact, you will not need to come up with more faith than you already have, if indeed, you have faith. You will not need to run to those who claim to have the inside track on how to build your faith.

FAITH IS NEVER A MATTER OF SIZE!

The solution to the disciples' problem is not a proportional increase in the size of their faith, but their commitment to obedience as a result of understanding their position in God's economy. The Lord tells a story to illustrate this point. A slave, having worked all day in the hot fields, does not come home to a meal cooked by his master. Rather, he comes home and immediately prepares his master's supper. Only after serving the master is the slave finally free to look after his own needs. Through all of this, the master does not thank the slave for his work. To this story our Lord compares the plight of the apostles. The work of forgiveness is their business, and having worked all day at it, they will receive no special commendation or thanks. They have done only what they were supposed to do.

Please notice that the Lord corrects the apostles on two fronts. He corrected them concerning the nature of faith and He corrected them concerning forgiveness, both of which are grace-based requirements for all disciples.

If the size of faith is never an issue, but at the same time many passages of Scripture seem to teach either the need for incremental increases in one's faith or that certain individuals have achieved such incremental increases, how are we to understand those passages? Let's look at them.

'Great Faith'

A look at the only two passages where our Lord commends both a man and a woman for their "great faith" supports our conclusion that the issue is never the size of one's faith. Rather, references to either "great faith" or "little faith" are dealing with the addition of or lack of truth one brings to a particular issue.

"Great faith" would mean believing certain things about God that most people, even the most regenerate ones, do not believe. It is not that people who believe such truths are more fervent in their faith (for example, in Jesus' deity or in His granting of eternal life to believers). It is that they believe advanced or deeper things about God and they allow those things to influence their convictions about God and His will in a particular situation. Let's look at the three places in the Gospels where the expression "great faith" occurs.

Matthew 8:10

The first occurrence takes place in Matthew 8:10 (see the parallel second occurrence in Luke 7:9). There the text makes mention of a centurion who was a military leader in charge of one hundred men. This Gentile came to Jesus (first having sent his friends to ask Him)[9] and asked Him to heal his servant. When Jesus said, "I will come and heal him," the centurion believed Him. But that is not what draws Jesus' remark about great faith. The context states,

> But the centurion replied, "Lord, I am not worthy to have you come under my roof. Instead, just say the word and my servant will be healed. For I too am a man under authority, with soldiers under me. I say to this one, 'Go' and he goes, and to another 'Come' and he comes, and to my slave 'Do this' and he does it."

What would most people do in this situation? They would not think of suggesting anything else, perhaps out of joy that the Lord had consented to go and heal the servant. Maybe they wouldn't even have conceived of the idea of healing from afar. But by his actions and words, this Gentile shows that he operates in a world of reason and order.

Notice the pattern of the centurion's response. First, he expresses his heart attitude of humility. This is the opposite of his vocational position in society. Unlike the Jews who believed that they were entitled to God's blessings, this man trusts that God will act out of mercy.

Second, the centurion expresses confidence that Jesus need only say "a word" and results are assured. The translation in the NET Bible has the definite article. However, in the original Greek it is just the word λόγος ("logos"). Because of the context, we understand that the "word" required was that his servant be healed.

It is critical that we understand the centurion's reasoning in verse 9, for only then can we fully appreciate why the Lord praises this man's faith. The centurion's response has to do with authority and obedience. The verse begins with "for" (*gar*), which indicates that a reason follows for the essence of what was said in verse 8. The reason Jesus can merely say a "word" and the centurion's servant will be healed is because Jesus has authority over sickness. When Jesus speaks, sickness has no other choice but to obey.

Third, the centurion tells the Lord Jesus that he knows He can heal the servant without going to his home. Jesus neither needs to see nor touch the servant for healing to take place.

Our Lord's response is instructive: "I tell you the truth, I have not found such faith in anyone in Israel!" (Matt. 8:10). The "great faith" is the centurion's belief that healing has nothing to do with distance. The Lord's authority is not just within the vicinity of His person. He commands, and it is done regardless of where the problem is. Clearly, the centurion's understanding of the Lordship of Jesus Christ was both wide and deep.

He did not just believe that Jesus could heal his servant of sickness. He understood the physical condition that required healing. He understood the authority that could bring about healing. He understood the relationship between healer and that which must be altered in order for perfect health to be restored. Where the centurion got his information is not clear. However, as a military officer in the Roman army, he worked with commands both from his superiors and those under him. Perhaps he drew a parallel from his own experience by extending it to include the Lord.

Therefore, let us be clear. The man is commended for his faith not because he had, over time, incrementally increased his belief about Jesus' ability to heal. Rather, he is commended because he had added to his belief system convictions that applied to his present situation. He believed that Jesus could heal his servant. He believed that healing was a matter of authority, which Jesus had over all things. He also believed that a simple command was necessary. In addition, he believed that healing had nothing to do with proximity. Missing these textual details has led many to draw incorrect conclusions about this and other passages.

Matthew 15:28

The final reference to "great faith" occurs in Matthew 15:28. This is the only other reference to the "great faith" of an individual commended by the Lord. After a Canaanite woman stopped the Lord Jesus and requested healing for her demon-possessed daughter, Jesus said, "I was sent only to the lost sheep of the house of Israel" (v. 24). The woman did not allow the Lord's subtle rebuff to deter her determination to receive healing for her child. She reacted by falling down before Him in an act of humility, asking, "Lord, help me."

The Lord again responds with a rebuff. However, this time, not as subtle as before. He declares, "It is not right to take the children's bread and throw it to the dogs" (v. 26). Again, the woman was not dissuaded. Her response is insightful. She said, "Yes, Lord. . . but even the dogs eat the crumbs that fall from their master's table" (v. 27). As if playing chess, the woman countered the Lord's rebuffs with truth. Does Jesus have another move, or is it checkmate?

The final response of the woman drew an unexpected response from the Lord: "Woman, your faith is great! Let what you want be done for you" (v. 28). This woman's faith has the same earmarks as the centurion's. First, she had "great faith" because she believed more than the mere fact that Jesus could heal her daughter. Second, she believed that the basis of His willingness to heal was mercy. Third, she held the conviction that God cares about all His creation, not just the Jews. This was clearly not the attitude of the Jewish disciples. They opposed the woman from the very beginning by instructing Jesus to "send her away, because she keeps crying out after us" (v. 23).

Thus, we see in the two examples where our Lord commends the faith of two Gentiles, each following the person's unexpected, insightful glimpse of God and His ways. Clearly, "great faith" is not about the size of faith, but the number of truths that informs one's confidence in God concerning a particular issue. "Great faith" understands that God works with man on the basis of mercy and not any sense of entitlement. It also understands that God as creator is free to do what He wants, any way He wants, whenever He wants.

"Great faith" is not about the incremental increase of faith as if one is filling a cup. Rather, "great faith" is filling a cup with truths. It is cutting up the pie into distinct truths that have a bearing on a particular situation. The more truths in that cup (or slices of the pie) as it relates to a particular situation, the greater one's faith. The opposite is equally true. This is the meaning of passages where our Lord rebukes men for "little faith."

'Little Faith'

At this point, I can imagine many readers raising their hands and asking about all those passages that state clearly that our Lord's disciples had "little faith." If there are no degrees of faith, how can the disciples have little faith?

The Greek word used is *oligōpistos* ("little faith"). It does not appear in classical Greek or in the LXX. Perhaps the Lord Jesus coined the term. It is only used five times in the entire New Testament. In each of those five occurrences, the issue is not a need for an incremental increase in faith concerning some proposition the apostles already believed, but the need for the apostles to expand the number of truths they can bring to bear on a particular situation. They needed to expand their knowledge base about God as it relates to a specific situation.

Only one of the passages in this category is really necessary to establish the factual basis of our claim. At the same time, the particular truth absent from the disciples' appreciation of God is worth the extra space in this book. Let us take a look at each passage and offer insight concerning how the disciples could have responded in order to have ensured a commendation from the Lord Jesus.

Matthew 6:30

"And if this is how God clothes the wild grass, which is here today and tomorrow is tossed into the fire to heat the oven, won't he clothe you even more, you people of little faith?"

Matthew 6:30 is part of an extended discussion in the Sermon on the Mount on exercising complete dependency on God for food, clothing, shelter, and water. The Lord draws several analogies between God's care for nature and His care for man, the crown of His creation. He first mentions God's care for the birds that neither sow nor reap nor gather into barns. The teaching is that God feeds the birds, but man is more important than birds. Jesus then turns to the flowers of the field. To produce their beauty, flowers do not work hard. The implication is that God looks after them to see that the fields are covered with beauty. He makes the point that man is more important than flowers and fields. Therefore, worrying about clothing evidences "little faith."

The issue concerned the disciples' need to believe something else about God as it related to their immediate circumstances. Their "little faith" did not include their belief that the Father would meet their basic needs. Notice that the issue is a *lack of knowledge* and not some lesser *degree of faith*. It is not that the disciples had "little faith" in God, but it was not enough to get them over the hump, as it were. They needed to trust in Him to provide their needs. Remember, it only takes a mustard seed-sized faith to move mountains. They needed to expand their belief structure to include a few more things or categories with respect to their particular circumstances. The disciples undoubtedly believed that Jesus was a great teacher, perhaps even a prophet like Jeremiah, Elijah, or Elisha. They believed that God was going to get involved in the political matters of the world and give national Israel lordship over the nations. However, they did not believe that God cares for and exercises lordship over food, clothing, water, and shelter.

If the disciples had recognized that God requires faithful "followship," which binds Him to supply their most basic needs, they would have received from Jesus a commendation instead of a condemnation. The Lord's comments with respect to birds and flowers are very helpful. It gives us a pattern for how to reason (how to apply truth to our circumstances) our way to a conclusion about any circumstances that will allow us to trust God rather than to worry.

There are five primary truths that the Lord indicates about our basic necessities that will prevent anxiety. It is interesting that these five truths will serve us well during the Great Persecution, as well. First, Jesus indicates that life is more important than physical things. Second, God has built into creation the means by which all things are cared for. Third, worry cannot improve anything that is important. Fourth, we are to focus on what's really important to God and He will supply us with those things that we should consider unimportant. Fifth and finally, man is of more value to God than animals. If the disciples had applied these five truths to their circumstances, they would have received a commendation instead of a condemnation.

The more slices of truth one adds to his pie, the greater is his faith. Having "great faith" has far more to do with the content of what one knows than the incremental increase of one's confidence or convictions about a particular truth.

Matthew 8:26

But he said to them, "Why are you cowardly, you people of little faith?" Then he got up and rebuked the winds and the sea, and it was dead calm.

In a story involving Jesus and the disciples on the Sea of Galilee, the Lord again rebuked His disciples for their "little faith." In a panic, fearing that a storm would sink the boat, the disciples awakened Jesus, saying, "Lord, save us! We are about to die!" (v. 25). At this point, Jesus replied, "Why are you cowardly, you people of little faith?" (v. 26). Then Jesus immediately stilled the winds and the waves, which filled the disciples with utter amazement (vv. 26–27).

Two important items in the Lord's response will help us understand the meaning of His remarks. The reference to "little faith" here concerns the disciples' failure to bring more than one truth to bear on their present circumstances. If the disciples wanted to be commended by Jesus in this situation, they needed to have had more categories in their understanding of the will of God. They needed to believe that God's plan for both them and Jesus would never suffer termination by an accident of nature. They needed to believe that God had the ability to keep them safe because Jesus was asleep on the boat. God was not about to allow his Son to die in this way. Their "little faith" involved only the conviction that if we awaken Jesus, He will save us.

The Lord accuses the disciples of acting "cowardly." The Greek noun *deilos* appears twice in the New Testament. The second reference is Revelation 21:8, where it appears in a list of people destined to spend eternity in the lake of fire.

On two occasions in the LXX, this word is used to describe people unwilling to fight in war. In Deuteronomy 19, Moses explains to the people

God's law concerning war with their enemies. On the occasion that people must fight, the priest would come before the soldiers and rehearse the attitude necessary for victory. The priest would instruct the soldiers to be courageous because God "goes with you to fight on your behalf against your enemies to give you victory" (Deut. 20:4).

Following the admonition by the priest, the officers of the troops were to dismiss all fighters (1) who were yet to dedicate newly built homes, (2) who had newly planted vineyards but were yet to reap a harvest, (3) who were newly engaged but were yet to consummate their vows, and finally (4) who were "afraid and fainthearted" (cowardly), lest they cause others to lose courage.

A similar context occurs in Judges 7. There, Gideon was instructed to reduce the ranks of those who would go out to fight against the Midianites. The Lord God was concerned that Gideon had too many men, which would result in the people thinking they had won the battle and not the Lord. Thus, the Lord instructs Gideon, "Now, announce to the men, 'Whoever is shaking with fear may turn around and leave Mount Gilead'" (Judges 7:3). The text reports that twenty-two thousand men went home. In both cases, the undesirables were described as those who were or who acted "cowardly."

In both Revelation 21:8 and these two Old Testament passages, our term occurs in a military context. However, in all cases, men were mere spectators as God was the primary agent responsible for the defeat of the enemy.

That our Lord used this unique term in Matthew 8:26 to describe the conduct of His disciples is not an accident. While the disciples probably did not have sufficient knowledge of the Old Testament to catch the relationship between their situation and that of the audience of Moses and Gideon, we do!

The reason the Lord rebukes His disciples' cowardly conduct is because it resulted from their "little faith." Their knowledge bank did not have several critical pieces necessary to deal with this particular situation. Because God was with them, they should have known that they were in no danger. Equally, they should have taken authority over the enemy (fear) or relaxed in the boat to see just how God would deal with this situation. They did not have the strength of conviction to calmly respond to their circumstances with truth. The first truth: God's Son is in the boat; therefore, it will not sink. The second truth: God's Son did not come into the world to die in a boat because of a storm. The third truth: Nothing in nature should frighten believers (fear is not of God). The fourth truth: Believers can face death in God's will with joy.

Matthew 14:31

Immediately Jesus reached out his hand and caught him, saying to him, "You of little faith, why did you doubt?"

The next example occurs in Matthew 14:31. When Jesus comes walking on the water, the disciples mistakenly take Him for a ghost (v. 26). After the Lord identifies Himself, Peter asks, "If it is you, order me to come to you on the water" (v. 28). After Jesus says, "Come," Peter gets out of the boat, walks on the water, and comes toward Jesus (v. 29). Then Peter breaks ranks, for the text states, "But when he saw the strong wind he became afraid. And starting to sink, he cried out, 'Lord, save me!'" (v. 30).

Immediately, we see the problem. The difference between "little faith" and "great faith" is knowledge of God's Word and ways, which come to bear on a given situation or circumstance. Peter got caught up in the moment, but once reality set in, his shallow knowledge base became apparent.

Jesus said, "O you [singular, speaking to Peter only] of little faith [singular], why did you [singular] doubt?" Peter's faith was little in this case because he got out of the boat with too few doctrinal convictions. Jesus rebukes Peter for his inadequate chest of doctrinal beliefs. As long as Peter's focus was on the Lord, he had no problems. Once he began to watch the waves, he began to doubt.

If Peter wanted to be commended for having great faith, he needed to believe that just as Jesus allowed him to get out of the boat to safety, Jesus would keep him until he got back in the boat. To that, he needed to add the conviction that safety is never a matter of one's external environment.

When people think they are safe, they are often in great danger. If Peter had in his arsenal the belief that whatever or whomever kept Jesus from sinking would also keep *him* from sinking, Peter would have received acclaim from the Lord instead of a rebuke.

Peter did not need an incremental increase in the size of his faith. Peter needed to add more items of conviction to his knowledge bank. God created all things, including the laws that govern nature. As such, He is able set them aside or suspend them for one second, one hour, one day, one year, or forever. If cessation of the waves was not necessary for Peter to walk on the water initially, the same was not necessary for him to continue doing so.

Matthew 16:8

When Jesus learned of this, he said, "You who have such little faith! Why are you arguing among yourselves about having no bread?"

Matthew 16:8 contains the Lord's final reference to "little faith" on the part of His disciples. (Parenthetically, it should be clear at this point that our Lord only used this phrase with the Twelve.) This particular rebuke follows an event during which He fed four thousand people with seven loaves of bread and a few small fish. Between this event and the Lord's rebuke, Matthew records a confrontation between the Lord and the Pharisees and Sadducees regarding whether Jesus would perform a sign sufficient to prove His identity.

It is following this event that the Lord warns the disciples about the leaven of the Pharisees and the Sadducees. As was their custom, the disciples totally misunderstood what He was talking about regarding leaven. They concluded that the Lord was upset about their having only one loaf of bread in the boat with them (see Mark 8:14).

The rebuke regarding their "little faith" leads to comments by our Lord about His feeding of the multitudes with plenty of food left over. In fact, when He fed the four thousand plus, there were seven baskets full of leftovers. When He fed the five thousand, there were twelve baskets full of leftovers. It is clear that the disciples should have learned from the seven baskets that God supplies perfectly and by the twelve baskets that God supplies superabundantly.

They had incontestable evidence that Jesus could meet their needs under any circumstances. The fact that they had one loaf with them should have been sufficient not to worry about bread. After questioning them about the leftovers, Jesus asks, "How could you not understand that I was not speaking to you about bread? But beware of the yeast of the Pharisees and Sadducees!" Matthew then adds the note that what the Lord was really talking about was "the teaching of the Pharisees and Sadducees."

Obviously, what "little faith" the disciples had in Jesus did not include the conviction that He would provide their daily bread. Their knowledge that He had miraculously fed the five thousand with so little was not influencing their conviction that He could feed twelve with one loaf.

If the disciples wanted to be recognized as possessing "great faith," they should have immediately believed that a lack of bread should never have been an issue of concern. They should have believed that God is a bread specialist. He had already ably demonstrated this. They should have believed that Jesus could call down manna from heaven or cause a fish to jump into the boat with money in its mouth to buy bread. Bread supply was not an issue for the God, who *is* bread (John 6:33). Their "little faith" lacked the doctrinal sophistication. At least one of the disciples should have had the presence of mind to say, "I may not know what the Lord is talking about, but I know for a fact that it isn't whether we forgot to bring loaves of bread."

We believe it is patently clear that "great faith" and "little faith" do not differ as to whether one has incrementally increased his faith about a truth or proposition. Rather, these terms have to do with whether one has the doctrinal sophistication to handle the circumstances that arise. "Great faith" means a person knows what truths or convictions to bring to bear on a particular situation.

As an example, let's take the all too real possibility that the country goes into a deep and extended recession. Companies are announcing layoffs. Cost of living is skyrocketing. Your monthly expenses are exceeding $3,500 a month. You lose your job. You have less than $500 in your saving account. How would a great faith handle this situation?

If one wants to exercise great faith in this context, he or she would need to bring several critical truths to bear. First, economic downturns have absolutely nothing to do with God's ability to supply our needs. Elijah and three-and-a-half years of drought is our illustration. Second, assuming that everyone around you knows that you are a committed Christian, God's reputation is on the line. Moses' reminder to God that the failure of His people to succeed opens the way for ridicule by the heathens is our illustration. Third, believers are to seek first God's righteousness and God takes care of our needs. The Apostle Paul's shipwreck and subsequent deliverance is our illustration. The final truth necessary to combat worry over a recession is this: God always supplies our needs in unexpected ways. That the Lord paid His and the disciples' taxes by finding the money in the mouth of a fish is our illustration.

Great faith has everything to do with knowledge and very little to do with the size of one's faith as a metaphysical reality. Education makes faith great and not some effort to turn mustard seeds into avocado seeds. One does not need a seminar on growing his or her faith, but a class on learning the doctrines of God's word.

Can Belief and Unbelief Co-Exist?

In Chapter 9 of Mark's gospel, there is a situation in which, during the absence of the Lord Jesus and three of His disciples, the remaining nine were in a heated debate regarding their inability to cast a demon out of a little boy. As soon as Jesus and the other disciples returned from the Mount of Transfiguration, they learned of the problem. Jesus becomes displeased with the nine because they were unable to heal the little boy. After the Lord inquired about the situation, He asked the boy's father, "How long has this been happening to him?" The man's reply is insightful. Having gotten no help from the nine disciples, the father was not sure that Jesus could help, either. Notice the dialogue between the man and Jesus at this point. The man reports,

> "It has often thrown him into fire or water to destroy him. But if you are able to do anything, have compassion on us and help us." Then Jesus said to him, "'If you are able?' All things are possible for the one who believes." Immediately the father of the boy cried out and said, "I believe; help my unbelief!"

The critical phrase is the last thought expressed in verse 24: "I believe; help my unbelief!" What did the man mean by this statement? It clearly cannot mean: "Lord I believe; help me because I don't believe." Yet, this is what it must mean if we take the traditional view that faith has incremental abilities to be either increased or decreased with regard to a truth. In other words, the man was persuaded that Jesus could heal his son, while at the same time, he was persuaded that Jesus could not heal his son.

The request for *help* in "help my unbelief" (v. 24) is the same verb the man uses earlier, "*Help* us" (v. 22). However, the very fact that the man approached Jesus with the words, "If you can do anything" shows that he was tentative. There is no doubt that the man wanted help. Evidently, the fact that Jesus' disciples had been unable to heal his son had thrown him into doubt about whether Jesus could help him, either. Then, when Jesus spoke with authority and repeated the man's words back to him, *If you are able*, with a tone of voice that indicated dismay that the man would doubt Him, the man's doubts vanished and he believed again that Jesus could heal his son. The man believed at that moment, but he realized that his belief was fragile and that he might fall into doubt once again.

The man's state of mind is understandable. He asked the disciples to heal his son and they were unable to do so. His confidence or conviction had taken a beating. His dialog with the Lord required him to reevaluate his understanding of Jesus and His relationship to the disciples. The man insulted Jesus by questioning His ability to heal. By repeating the phrase, "If you are able," the Lord forced the man to refocus and understand that He was not just one of the boys. The important point is, the man did not have a "little faith" to which he needed to add a "little more" in order to have enough faith for Jesus to perform a miracle. Rather, the man vacillated from belief to unbelief and back to belief.

Conclusion

The difference between "great faith" and "little faith" is not a matter of incremental increases concerning one's convictions about something. Rather, it is how many convictions one can bring to bear on the matter.

This should be of great comfort to us as we consider the matter of surviving the great persecution of Satan and his Antichrist. One will not need to manufacture a "super faith" so as to walk with God during this time. Rather, he or she will need to have solid convictions developed from a deep and wide knowledge of God and His Word.

Faith: Does It Have Degrees?

We shall develop this matter in our discussion of Hebrews 11, which follows later in this book.

---

[1]*Journal of the Grace Evangelical Society Vol. 19*, vnp.19.37.3 (The Grace Evangelical Society, 2006; 2007).

[2] *Bibliotheca Sacra Vol. 132*, 132:345 (Dallas Theological Seminary, 1975; 2002).

[3] *Bibliotheca Sacra Vol. 132*, 132:346 (1975; 2002).

[4]Horst Robert Balz and Gerhard Schneider, *Exegetical Dictionary of the New Testament*, Translation of: Exegetisches Worterbuch zum Neuen Testament., 3:65 (Grand Rapids, Mich.: Eerdmans, 1990-c1993).

[5] The next reference to the belief of the disciples concerns an event in the earlier ministry of our Lord, but the disciples discerned the significance of it only after His resurrection. Thus, it does not directly bear on our discussion.

[6]Gerald L. Borchert, John 12–21, *The New American Commentary, New International Version*, Vol. 25B (Nashville: Broadman & Holman, 2002), 89.

[7] *Journal of the Grace Evangelical Society Vol. 19*, vnp.19.37.7–19.37.8 (The Grace Evangelical Society, 2006; 2007).

[8]Horst Robert Balz and Gerhard Schneider, *Exegetical Dictionary of the New Testament*, translation of: *Exegetisches Worterbuch zum Neuen Testament*, 3:177 (Grand Rapids, Mich.: Eerdmans, 1990–c1993).

[9] See Zane C. Hodges, "The Centurion's Faith in Matthew and Luke," *Bibliotheca Sacra* (October–December 1964). Hodges harmonizes the Matthean and Lukan accounts.

Chapter 8

Faith Versus a Lack of History

Matthew 21:21

Jesus answered them, "I tell you the truth, if you have faith and do not doubt, not only will you do what was done to the fig tree, but even if you say to this mountain, 'Be lifted up and thrown into the sea,' it will happen." (NET)

Jesus answered them, "Of a truth I say to you all, if you all should have faith and you all are not given to playing the middle, not only will you all do this type of thing to a fig tree, but should you all say to the mountain, 'be lifted up and cast into the sea,' it shall happen.

(author's translation)

Historically, the simple sense of Matthew 21:21 has been taken to mean "doubt," which is seen as the opposite of faith. According to this view, the reason so many believers are not witnessing the miraculous works of God is because of doubt. The text as much says so! Therefore, it would seem that if one wants to see those miraculous works intimated in Matthew 21:21, a person must learn to trust God and not doubt. It seems very simple.

Yet, most believers cannot seem to figure out this formula for their personal success. If the verse is so simple, then we must conclude that the overwhelming majority of believers simply doubt the power of God and thus are not personally witnessing His miraculous works. Can it really be that simple? If doubt is the real problem, then why are so many people unable to overcome it?

We believe the real problem is an incorrect translation, which leads to an incorrect interpretation, which naturally leads an incorrect application. The result? Not many mountains are being moved these days, even among those who supposedly teach us as experts about faith!

Diakrinō (διακρίνω), the Greek verb that stands behind the English translation, is not cut and dry when it comes to the best possible nuance intended by New Testament authors. This verb occurs nineteen times in the New Testament.[1] The following chart reflects the differences in translation of the term in the NET Bible:

Reference	The NET Bible
Matthew 16:3	To judge
Matthew 21:21	Do not doubt
Mark 11:23	Does not doubt
Acts 10:20	Without hesitation
Acts 11:2	Took issue with
Acts 11:12	Without hesitation
Acts 15:9	Made no distinction
Romans 4:20	Waver in unbelief
Romans 14:23	Who doubts
1 Corinthians 4:7	Concedes
1 Corinthians 6:5	To settle disputes
1 Corinthians 11:29	Without careful regard
I Corinthians 11:31	Examined
1 Corinthians 14:29	Evaluate
James 1:6a, 6b	Without doubting or Who doubts
James 2:4	Made distinctions
Jude 9, 22	Arguing with or Those who waver

One immediately notices the difference in how scholars translate the Greek verb into English. The most popular contemporary translations of Matthew 21:21 encourage the average believer to take the text as it stands. However, a little investigation about the meaning of the Greek term translated "doubt" reveals a problem. It becomes very clear that New Testament scholars have given this word several nuances. A check of Greek lexicons reveals that this term generally means to "differentiate," "decide," and "judge" in an active sense. It generally means to "dispute with one another," "estimate," "explain," "interpret" and "doubt" as a non-active sense or as the Greeks would express it a middle verb.

Who determined the meaning of this two-thousand-year-old biblical term? There were very few, if any, lexicons at the time this text was written. How do we know that the meaning of this and other ancient terms indicated in our modern lexicons is right? Primarily, we utilize all the manuscripts found throughout the past two thousand years. By collecting these documents and painstakingly going through each page, we build a list of the possible ways a particular word was used. The differing contexts in which the word appears set the range of possible nuances assigned to it. It is therefore of great interest to us that concerning *diakrinō* and the translation "to doubt," *The Theological Dictionary of the New Testament* concludes: "This meaning. . . is not known prior to the N.T."[2] In other words, there is no evidence that this verb was ever used to mean "to doubt" before New Testament translators began the practice 200 plus years after the New Testament was written.

As a result of an exhaustive study of all known ancient literary writings from two hundred years before the writing of the New Testament books to one hundred years afterwards, David Degraaf concludes, "Nowhere... does any form of διακρίνω mean "doubt."[3] Degraaf found more than three hundred eighty examples of some form of *diakrinō* during this time period. Yet, not one clear, unmistakable, unambiguous example of this particular usage occurred.

This, in and of itself, does not prove that *diakrinō* did not come to mean "to doubt." However, it should cause us to pause. Is it possible that the translators missed the intending meaning of Matthew's text? When we compare Scripture with Scripture, we believe the answer is yes!

In Matthew 14:31, when our Lord chastises Peter for his "little faith," as illustrated by Peter's thinking that he would perish while Jesus stood by, Jesus asks, "Why did you start to doubt?" The Greek verb *distazō* is used. It occurs twice in the New Testament (Matt. 14:31, 28:17). It is correctly translated and means exactly what the English translation suggests. However, as one can see, it is not the word used in Matthew 21:21 and there is no evidence that the two terms are synonymous.

It is our belief that *distazō*, when used opposite faith, focuses on objective verifiable truth. For example, in Matthew 14:31, Peter had already proven that walking on water was possible. He saw the Lord doing it, and he did it, too. Yet, after the objective verifiable fact of his own experience, Peter started to doubt. The same can be said in Matthew 28:17. The objective verifiable truth of the Lord's resurrection had multiple attesting witnesses by the time the Lord met the eleven in Galilee. A large segment of the Jews believed in the resurrection from the dead. Yet some of them doubted what they saw with their own eyes — the Lord standing in their midst having been raised from the dead.

In contrast, *diakrinō* focuses on faithfulness as a character trait when used in connection with faith. In essence, rather than focusing on faith to move a mountain, the focus is on whether or not there has been a pattern of moving mountains. The emphasis is on faithfulness in other areas of one's life. To move mountains, one must have a record of faithfulness to God.

The closest chronological and theological parallel to Matthew 21:21 is James 1:5-8. Both were written within a ten-year period of the other. *Diakrinō* occurs three times in this book. The first instance of the term occurs in James 1:6. The verse reads, "But he must ask in faith without doubting, for the one who doubts are like a wave of the sea, blown and tossed around by the wind." *Diakrinō* occurs twice in this verse, and the NET Bible translates both instances with a form of the verb "to doubt." This translation is consistent with most other translations. Since the term occurs opposite faith (*pistis*), this passage serves as an important parallel to help shed light on the meaning of Matthew 21:21.

To doubt something or someone basically means to be uncertain. Dictionary.com defines the core notion of uncertainty in multiple ways. Uncertainty does not seem to be the issue in Matthew.

If James is arguing that the opposite of a man of faith is a man who doubts, then he has effectively doomed his audience to a state of hopelessness. James indicates that God will not give the doubter any help whatsoever. James states, "That man [the doubter] should not think he will receive anything from the Lord." How can he move from the sphere of doubt to the sphere of faith unless he receives help from God? The doubter is labeled "double-minded" and "unstable." This state makes self-deliverance impossible. If God requires complete single-mindedness (stable thinking) prior to asking for wisdom but the person does not have this capacity, then such a man has no remedy.

Fortunately, this conclusion is contradicted by the very ministry of Jesus Christ. As stated earlier, Jesus identified Peter as a doubter. Yet, the Lord specifically did miracles to convince Peter and others of His assertions. The hopeless state of the doubter and our Lord's ministry to convince doubters to believe seem to argue against the traditional translation and interpretation of *diakrinō* in James 1:6–9.

Therefore, we believe *diakrinō* must have some other sense in this text. God's obvious goal is the faithfulness of His people. One who is faithful to God's rules and regulations can expect to receive wisdom from God so that he might continue to please Him. One must therefore be able to achieve this status. Otherwise, he will never be able to ask wisdom from God.

James' Influence on Matthew 21:21

There is some agreement among scholars that after greeting his readers,

> James introduces the themes of his letter. As in many Greek letters intended for publication, he doubles his opening, introducing his main themes first in 1:2–11 and then again (with an advance in development) in 1:12–27.[4]

Peter H. Davids agrees. He writes, "James presents the first statement of his main themes in 1:2–11.[5] If this assessment is correct, then the Book of James will have three major themes: woes, wisdom, and wealth. These are the concerns expressed in the first eleven verses of the first chapter of this book. Since *diakrinō* occurs in verse six, we are directly concerned with the major theme of the verses that cover it. Davids understands James 1:2–4 to deal with testing. James 1:5–8 covers wisdom, and James 1:9–11 deal with wealth.[6] Therefore, we are directly concerned with the theme of wisdom.

James introduces the topic of wisdom in chapter one. Verses 5–8 state:

> But if anyone is deficient in wisdom, he should ask God, who gives to all generously and without reprimand, and it will be given to him. But he must ask in faith without doubting, for the one who doubts is like a wave of the sea, blown and tossed around by the wind. For that person must not suppose that he will receive anything from the Lord, since he is a double-minded individual, unstable in all his ways.

It would seem that James believes that the correct response to the various trials believers face is wisdom. Not just any wisdom, but the wisdom that comes from God. Those who find themselves devoid of God's wisdom can ask for it with the assurance that He will provide it as long as the request is faith-based.

The term "faith" (*pistis*) is typically translated "faith" here. The idea seems to be that God will only honor the requests of those who ask in faith or with confidence that God will answer their request. The traditional notion that any doubt about God's willingness to answer will be met with His ready refusal seems to challenge common sense. While such conduct is rightly required of those who have matured in Christ, it is difficult to see how new believers could live up to such a standard.

As we demonstrated earlier, the size of one's faith does not have an impact on whether or not the mountain moves. It only takes a mustard seed of faith to see great works done. Therefore, we have trouble with the idea that only requests surrounded by confidence that God will answer "yes" have any chance of receiving a positive response. Even the Lord Jesus prayed with doubt about God's answer to His prayer. When we look at our Lord the night before His crucifixion, He prays for the Father to give Him another option other than death on a cross. Our Lord is asking for something He knows He cannot have. He cannot be confident that God will answer in the affirmative. In fact, the Lord knows that His Father cannot answer His prayer.

When one is struggling to trust God in a particular matter and prays for God's help to believe, if we take the traditional view, that person should not expect any help at all. Only *after* becoming confident of God's help should one pray for that help. Yet, Scripture has an example that clearly contradicts this conclusion. In the case of Moses, God worked with and through him to deliver the children of Israel when the Scriptures clearly portray Moses as one who doubted both himself and God.

We conclude that the traditional interpretation of James 1:5-8 runs askew of the general tenor of Scripture. If the doubter must stop doubting before he can request help from God, then he is left to overcome his problems without any help from God. It would seem to us that the traditional interpretation that assigns the meaning "to doubt" to *diakrinō* is not correct.

Of interest to this discussion is Paul's remark in Romans 4:20 regarding Abraham. This verse reports, "He [Abraham] did not waver in unbelief about the promise of God but was strengthened in faith, giving glory to God." The phrase "did not waver" translates *diakrinō*. It is clear that the verb *diakrinō* cannot have the meaning "to doubt" here. However, the decision to translate the text "He did not waver in unbelief about the promise of God" (i.e. that God would give him a son long after both he and Sarah were unable to physical produce a child) is hard to understand given what we know about Abraham's story. In fact, Genesis 17:17–18 states, "Then Abraham bowed down with his face to the ground and laughed as he said to himself, "Can a son be born to a man who is a hundred years old? Can Sarah bear a child at the age of ninety? Abraham said to God, 'O that Ishmael might live before you!'"

Clearly, Abraham's laugh is the laugh of disbelief. Concerning the meaning of Abraham's action and the connection of Romans 4:20, one author writes, "It was not the sneer of unbelief, but a smile of delight at the improbability of the event" (Rom. 4:20).[7] Yet, the context clearly contradicts this conclusion. A similar episode involving the laugh of unbelief follows in Genesis 18:12–15. There as here, when confronted, Sarah lied. We know she lied because there was something wrong with her laugh. It was not the laugh of wonderment, but the laugh of unbelief (see Luke 24:42).

The reality of Abraham's situation contradicts the translation suggested in Romans 4:20. He did indeed waver in unbelief about God's fulfillment of the promise of a special progeny. Therefore, some other translation is necessary to reflect Abraham's true behavior.

As we suggested earlier, *diakrinō* focuses on faithfulness as a character trait when used opposite faith. In this sense, Abraham continued to do the works of faith regardless of whether there were periodic lapses in judgment. Therefore, we would suggest a translation that reads, "He did not continually remain neutral concerning the promise of God through unbelief. . ." In other words, Abraham did experience periods of neutrality when he vacillated between belief and unbelief. He refused to pick a side. He refused to distinguish between trusting God and trying to fix the problem himself. He did do these things, but this conduct did not become his continual lifestyle.

The image of a man staggering from side to side perfectly reflects the intended meaning of *diakrinō*. Instead of making a decision to move forward, the person acts like a yo-yo or the ball in a video game. He is in constant motion, but not moving in a positive way. In essence, this person runs in a circle between two goals. Therefore, it is not doubt, but what doubt produces that is the problem. Doubt produces indecision, a leaning from side to side like an oscillating fan that continually sweeps the room. Thus, "He [Abraham] did not exist in a state the result of staggering in unbelief with regards to the promise of God, but he grew stronger in belief." The idea is best expressed in the statement that Abraham was moving forward, just not in a straight line.

We find more support for this conclusion when we look at the comparative illustration used by James. He describes the person who should not expect any help from God to be (1) like a wave of the sea, blown and tossed around by the wind; and (2) double-minded, unstable in all his ways. Since most scholars agree that the two descriptive phrases say essentially same thing, the most important question is this: "What is the point of comparison?" The wind has two impacts on the wave of the sea. It causes the wave to be *blown* and *tossed around*. It is this effect that James describes as "a man of two minds." This is what the Greek literally says. James states that a double-minded man is "unstable in all his ways." *Akatastatos* (ἀκατάστατος) is consistently translated "unstable" in the majority of English translations. A.T. Robertson concludes, "It means unsteady, fickle, staggering, reeling like a drunken man.[8]

The Greek word for "unstable" occurs only in the New Testament in the Book of James (1:8 and 3:8). In James 3:8, the text states, "It [the tongue] is a *restless* evil" (ESV, NASB, NIV). The KJV translates it *unruly*. That James uses the term again in chapter three is important in light of the fact that this chapter expands his discussion of the theme first introduced in 1:5–8. Just as in chapter one, the third chapter offers several illustrations with doublets. Notice the chart below:

	Wave of the Sea	
Blown		Tossed Around
	Double-Minded	
One Mind		Another Mind
	Tongue	
Bless		Curse
	Fresh Water Spring	
Fresh Water		Bitter Water
	Fig Tree	
Figs		Olives
	Vine	
Grapes		Figs
	Salt Water Spring	
Salt Water		Fresh Water

The table above reflects James' love for doublets that illustrate the unnatural conduct often evident in nature—unnatural conduct that God finds undesirable in His children. With the exception of the "wave of the sea," each of the remaining six doublets manifests conduct inconsistent with its basic nature. Salt water springs should produce salt water and fresh water springs should produce fresh water. Fig trees should produce figs and vines should produce grapes. That two extremes are traced to the same source contradicts common sense. This is James' point. Just as salt water springs should only produce salt water, followers of God should produce righteousness consistently. Otherwise, the righteous bounce between to opinions: trust or distrust. *Diakrinō* describes this process.

Because James uses the doublet illustration in both chapters one and three, we feel strongly that his point in chapter one is not the instability of a double-minded man, but such a man's lack of devotion to one way of life. He is not committed to either. His commitment is to remain in an unruly state, vacillating from side to side, such as from belief to unbelief. He believes for some things, but does not believe for others.

This emphasis is in accord with the basic meaning of *diakrinō*. The problem with this man is not doubt, but his preference for continued living in an unruly state. He is not totally ruled by God or the world. He refuses to make a *distinction* between either, but treats them the same. He is disloyal, but attempts to use either for his own good. That an idea closer to *distinctions* is better finds support in James 2:4, which states, "If so, have you not made *distinctions* among yourselves and become judges with evil motives?" The decision to translate *diakrinō* "to make distinction" is well founded here.

There are those who insist that "to doubt" is the meaning of *diakrinō* here. However, the context is clearly against it. The basic core meaning involves the aspect of judging, i.e., to discern, distinguish, or differentiate. The fact that

James questions whether these people have "become judges with evil motives," argues strongly for the translation reflected in most Bible translations: "made distinctions" (NET, ESV, NASB, and RSV) and "discriminated" (NIV). The fact that James begins chapter two with a warning against *prejudice* or *partiality* (of a judicial nature), and the fact that verse 4 concludes that initial discussion supports our conclusion. That James would use the same word in such close proximity but intend two different meanings is possible. However, because the nuance in chapter one is suspect, it is more probable that James intends the same basic sense for both passages.

Given all that we have presented about the book of James, the better translation of *diakrinō* in James 1:6 is "to refuse to distinguish" or "to play the middle." Such a man moves to the left or right, but always comes back to the middle. We could thus translate James 1:6, "But ask out of the midst of faithfulness, in contrast to a life of playing the middle. For the one who plays the middle is like a wave of the sea, blown and tossed around by the wind." Giving *diakrinō* this sense better harmonizes the sense of the whole verse. While a doubter cannot receive anything from God to help remove his doubts, a person who plays the middle does not need anything from God to abandon his unruly state. He needs only to begin to walk in faithfulness. He needs only to choose God's side.

This understanding also makes sense in Matthew 21:21. If *diakrinō* means "to play the middle" in the sense that a person refuses to distinguish or judge between two options, then the sense of the text is this: "Jesus answered them, 'I tell you all the truth, if you all have a faithful life and you all are not given to playing the middle, not only will you all do what was done to the fig tree, but even if you all say to this mountain, 'Be lifted up and thrown into the sea,' it will happen."

Having clarified that the size of faith has nothing to do with how big the task is that needs to be done, it is evident that Matthew 21:21 cannot refer to the need for faith in an absolute sense. The disciples had at least a mustard-seed-sized faith in God. Their main problem was their insistence on playing the middle. They wanted to believe in Jesus, but only for those things they wanted. They only believed some of the things Jesus said and promised. They were not convinced of the total program. In a sense, they halted between two opinions — between belief and unbelief.

The primary reason we see so few miracles today is not because God has stopped doing them. The problem is that God finds very few people willing to declare war on the flesh and step out of the middle. We play the middle most of our lives. We have confidence in God for eternal life, but in everything else, we constantly choose sides between God's way and man's way. Man's way wins out most of the time. This vacillation between God's way on some things and man's way on others is exactly what Jesus was talking about in Matthew 21:21.

Most of us do not really understand just how much we live our lives vacillating back and forth between the two ways. Our whole American culture is set up to do it. For example, we would not think of living without insurance: health, life, car, home, flood, hurricane, dental, Social Security, and so on. Of course, the government demands that we must have some of these things. The problem is not having them, but the confidence we place that, once we have them, everything is going to be all right. However, that ultimately produces vacillation between total dependency on God and conditional dependency. The Bible describes it as *mā diakrinō.*

---

[1]Horst Robert Balz and Gerhard Schneider, *Exegetical Dictionary of the New Testament*, Translation of: *Exegetisches Worterbuch zum Neuen Testament*, 1:305 (Grand Rapids, Mich.: Eerdmans, 1990–c1993).

[2]*Theological Dictionary of the New Testament*, Vols. 5–9 edited by Gerhard Friedrich. Vol. 10 compiled by Ronald Pitkin., ed. Gerhard Kittel, Geoffrey William Bromiley and Gerhard Friedrich, electronic ed., 3:947 (Grand Rapids, MI: Eerdmans, 1964-c1976).

[3] *Journal of the Evangelical Theological Society Vol. 48,* vnp.48.4.736 (The Evangelical Theological Society, 2005; 2006).

[4]D. A. Carson, *New Bible Commentary: 21st Century Edition*, rev. ed. of *The New Bible Commentary*, third ed., edited by D. Guthrie, J.A. Motyer, 1970, fourth ed., James 1:1 (Leicester, England; Downers Grove, Ill., USA: Inter-Varsity Press, 1994).

[5]Peter H. Davids, *The Epistle of James: A Commentary on the Greek Text*, includes indexes (Grand Rapids, Mich.: Eerdmans, 1982), 65.

[6]Ibid.

[7]Robert Jamieson, A. R. Fausset, A. R. Fausset et al., *A Commentary, Critical and Explanatory, on the Old and New Testaments*, Gen. 17:17 (Oak Harbor, WA: Logos Research Systems, Inc., 1997).

[8]A.T. Robertson, *Word Pictures in the New Testament*, Vol. V © 1932, Vol. VI © 1933 by Sunday School Board of the Southern Baptist Convention, James 1:8 (Oak Harbor: Logos Research Systems, 1997).

Chapter 9

Faith: A Characterization

I f survival of the Great Persecution is the sovereign choice of God; and if (as we have demonstrated above) the size of faith is irrelevant to the quantity or quality of the works that faith can accomplish; and if "great faith" is composed of multiple truths from God's Word and ways brought to bear on a particular situation or circumstance; then what choice is left for you? Will you trust God in the midst of your circumstances to accomplish His perfect will in your life? Naturally, if you are a true follower of Jesus Christ, you want to answer in the affirmative!

However, we know that the real problem for any believer is not faith itself, since faith is a fixed quantity given by God, but knowledge. This means knowledge about how to trust God regardless of whatever He allows to happen during this unparalleled time. Whether starvation, imprisonment, or death, we must trust Him the same way believers have trusted Him down through the centuries. Fortunately, in His great mercy, God has given us clear examples in the Bible that picture how to walk in faith in the face of great trials and receive His praise and honor. Knowledge is the key!

We saw in James 1:5–8 instructions about how to acquire knowledge and wisdom. Again, God in His great mercy has given us illustrations of men and women who utilized godly knowledge and wisdom to deal with their present circumstances, ultimately winning victory and praise. When wisdom from God operates in the midst of our circumstances as God intended, this process is accurately described as a person *acting in great faith*. Hebrews 11 illustrates this conclusion. The men and women of this great chapter saw future events as incontrovertible evidence of God's faithfulness sufficient for them to act in obedience to God's will during their day. The greatest motivation for the present is the knowledge of God's promises for the future.

In this, we must follow in the footsteps of the Old Testament saints. We, too, must learn to see God's faithfulness in the events that will comprise biblical fulfillment long before those events literally come to pass—just as they did.

Stop and think about that statement. *We, too, must learn to see God's faithfulness in the events that will comprise biblical fulfillment long before those events literally come to pass.* What does it really mean? Once these prophetic events begin, instead of experiencing fear and deep foreboding, we must see their beginnings as confirmation of the faithfulness of God. God told us what would happen, and as each event begins to unfold, we have confirmation that He is faithful to His Word—all of it, whether good or bad from a human perspective.

Take, for example, the abomination of desolation or Antichrist's desecration of a Jewish worship site in Jerusalem. Most believers look at this event in a negative way because of the fear of physical persecution that will come with it. It can just as easily be seen as a positive confirmation of God's faithfulness to His Word and the key indicator that just three-and-a-half years remain before God takes back control of the earth and His people will live in and enjoy His presence forever! Once this event occurs, there will be no room for doubt about God and His plan.

These promised events should inspire faithfulness on our part, both now and when the events ultimately occur. This is the kind of faith the writer of Hebrews presents. It is faith that acts upon the communication of God (wisdom) in the present in light of the outcome of all future events. With the fulfillment of each promise, God confirms what we already know — that He is faithful — which should inspire more and more confidence in His yet unfulfilled promises about the eschatological future.

Long before the events depicted in Matthew 24 begin to occur, we must see proof of their fulfillment in the testimony of God recorded in the Bible almost two thousand years ago. By knowing what is going to happen, it should motivate us to an all-out effort to develop the knowledge necessary to act in such a way as to receive from Christ the commendation "great faith"!

How to Be Victorious

To understand the actions and attitudes of God's people that will be necessary to face and prove victorious over Satan and his Antichrist, we will turn our attention to a close examination of Hebrews 11. However, it will not be for the reasons most would think. This great chapter will teach us how to please God. Faith is the key, but not as generally understood.

Responding victoriously to the Great Persecution will require "great faith." This is a faith that is well informed with doctrinal sophistication, a faith that sees promise and fulfillment on the same level. In other words, it is faith that makes the fulfillment as certain as the promise — faith that makes it possible for a person to react to God's promises just as if one was experiencing the fulfillment. In other words, the promise is no less real than the fulfillment. This is not mental gymnastics or psychological hocus pocus. Rather, it is faith in action. Again, to understand this dynamic of faith and to see biblical examples, we turn to Hebrews 11.

If as we have demonstrated, the lexical or dictionary terms used throughout the New Testament define faith as "reliance" or "trust," then why does the author of Hebrews not follow this simple lexical way of defining the term? He could have just said that "faith" means reliance or trust in something or someone. Instead, as one commentator points out, "The two key words in the passage [Hebrews 11:1]. . . are "assurance" and "conviction," both indicating that faith is an attitude of certainty about some truth claim."[1] Yet, the writer of the epistle to the Hebrews is most eloquent, if anything at all. He is very able to express himself. Therefore, if as this commentator states, "Faith is an attitude of certainty about some truth claim," we expect the author of Hebrews to say it in unambiguous terms. Yet, this is not the case.

The author of Hebrews does not give the dictionary definition of faith. Rather, he characterizes faith by its conduct. He demonstrates that faith is the evidence for what cannot be seen because it has not yet occurred. Faith is not leaping from mountaintop to mountaintop with a deep valley between them. Faith is the solid bridge between mountaintops that allows believers to walk from one to the other.

We are not alone in our conclusion that Hebrews 11:1 is not a technical definition of faith. Gerald L. Borchert writes, "In reality Hebrews 11:1 is not a definition of faith but a paradoxical description of its effects."[2] Paul Ellingworth believes that "the verse is more or other than a definition."[3] S. M. Baugh[i] explains the reason many interpret Hebrews 11:1 to be a definition of faith. He writes,

> In large part, this common interpretation is inspired and reinforced by highly questionable traditional renderings of key terms. . . from Heb. 11:1-2, which continue on in newer English versions despite well-founded objections in lexical and scholarly authorities.[4]

In other words, interpreters follow the insistence of modern translations that "assurance" and "conviction" express the meaning of the two

---

[i] Most of the exegetical insights reflected in the following discussion of Hebrews 11:1-31 were taken from an article written by S. M. Baugh entitled "The Cloud of Witnesses in Hebrews 11." His article can be found in Libronix Digital Library System at *Westminster Theological Journal* Vol. 68, vnp.68.1.113 (Westminster Theological Seminary, 2006; 2007). However, the difference between his covenantal background and my dispensational background will be quickly evident.

terms in Hebrews 11:1. However, allow us to take a closer look at this pivotal text to see whether we can clarify its meaning and intent.

Hebrews 11

The importance of Hebrews 11 for surviving the persecution of Satan and his Antichrist cannot be overstated. The author of this great chapter writes to convince his readers that they have three important sources to champion their success: the inscripturated (written down) promises of God, the witness of notable Old Testament believers who illustrate how to act on God's promises, and the Lord Jesus. These are sufficient evidence that what God has promised concerning both the temporal (millennial) and eternal kingdoms is true and will come to pass. For any generation of believers struggling to persevere in the face of intense pressure, faith (the written word, the Old Testament witnesses, and the great Witness) is the evidence of promises yet to be fulfilled.

The author of Hebrews in chapter 11:1-40 presents case after case of individuals who acted on the basis of God's verbally expressed promises. Those promises were so certain to see fulfillment regardless of how long it might take that they became the evidence and basis of the actions of Old and New Testament saints. The only question that remains is this: will they become the basis of our actions if we are called upon to be that final generation.

Hebrews 11:1–2

The NET Bible: Now faith is being sure of what we hope for, being convinced of what we do not see. For by it the people of old received God's commendation.

ESV: Now faith is the assurance of things hoped for, the conviction of things not seen. For by it the people of old received their commendation.

NASB: Now faith is the assurance of things hoped for, the conviction of things not seen. For by it the men of old gained approval.

KJV: Now faith is the substance of things hoped for, the evidence of things not seen. For by it the elders obtained a good report.

A survey of modern translations of Hebrews 11:1 quickly reveals a subtle change from the earliest edition of the King James Version. While "assurance" (ESV) and "being sure" (NET) remain popular translations of *hupostasis* (ὑπόστασις, the Greek term), many in the scholarly community agree that these terms should not be translated this way. Rather, the sense reflected in the 1611

King James Version is a better translation of the original Greek.

What may appear as a very subtle difference in most English translations is really quite significant. The difference in meaning between "substance" and "assurance" is one of tangible perception. Notice that synonyms for "substance" are "matter," "materials," and "stuff." However, "assurance" has synonyms like "pledge," "declaration," and "oath." One speaks of that which is tangible, physical, and touchable in contrast to that which is subjective and non-corporeal.

The Greek term *hupostasis* was used in early medical texts for the sediment or accumulation that settled at the bottom of liquids. Clearly, in this sense, there is a tangible, objective substance in focus. In philosophy, it was often used to refer to real "substance," "essence," or "being" in a metaphorical way. S.M Baugh writes,

> The philosophical usage for *hupostasis* ("essence," "reality," "substance") is immediately relevant for Hebrews in that this is the universally accepted meaning in Heb. 1:3 where we read that the Son is the stamp (*charaktār*) of the divine "nature" (ESV; RSV; NASB), "being" (NIV; NAB), "very being" (NRSV; NKJV), "person" (KJV), ["essence" (NET)].[5]

The other use of *hupostasis* is in Hebrews 3:14. Here our term "parallels 'frankness' and 'pride in hope'" (see 3:6 and cf. 10:23, 35ff.) and refers to "resolve" or "point of departure."[6] These findings support *The Greek–English Lexicon of the New Testament and Other Ancient Near Eastern Languages* (p. 1041) position that, "The sense 'confidence,' 'assurance'. . . for Heb. 11:1 has enjoyed much favor but must be eliminated, since examples of it cannot be found."

Hence, as earlier stated, a better translation of Hebrews 11:1 was given in the earliest edition of the King James Version: "Now faith is the *substance* of things hoped for" (emphasis added). It is the tangible, hard reality of things hoped for in the future.

The second word that requires reexamination in Hebrews 11:1 is *elegchos* (ἔλεγχος), often translated in modern versions as "conviction" (ESV), "being convinced" (NET), or "being. . . certain" (NIV). This decision by most modern translations contradicts the early history of this term. A study reveals that it occurs most often in judicial contexts for the refutation or disproof of an argument or charge. Later, it came to mean an examination of the evidence, as well as the evidence or proof itself used to establish an argument or legal condemnation.

Finally, from the related verb *elegchō* (ἐλέγχω = "I reprove, rebuke"), the noun can also denote a reproof, which is its most frequent meaning in the LXX. S. M. Baugh concludes,

Beyond this, there is very little leeway for *elegchos*, and it never demonstrably signifies mental certainty as to the truth or reality of something as our versions indicate when they render *elegchos* as "conviction" (ESV; NASB; NRSV) or "being... certain" (NIV; TNIV).[7]

Translating *elegchos* properly leads to this somewhat confusing translation: "Now faith is...the evidence of things not seen" (KJV; cf. NKJV, NAB). Again, S. M. Baugh concludes,

As a result of this difficulty, James Moffatt posited that the author of Hebrews was giving *elegchos* a new meaning here: "Έλεγχος was used in a *fresh sense,* as the subjective 'conviction'. . . The writer could find no Greek term for the idea, and therefore struck out a *fresh application* for ἔλεγχος." However, the author of Hebrews did indeed have several other terms at hand in Greek by which to communicate the concept of mental "assurance," "confidence," or "conviction."[8]

We concur with Baugh that there is no need to follow Moffatt's conclusion here. Thus, "Now faith is the substance of what we hope for and the evidence of things not seen" correctly reflects the original author's intended meaning. The author is not talking about something that is subjective and thus left to each individual to conjure up in his or her own mind. Rather, faith can be characterized as an objective hard, fact when God's Word stands in back of it.

Wisdom From God

The third and final key word to reflect on in the first two initial verses of Hebrews 11 is *emarturāthāsan* (ἐμαρτυρήθησαν), which is rendered "received God's commendation." The verb *martureō* can indicate a positive testimony about someone in the sense of "to approve or praise." However, this is not the intended meaning for Hebrews 11:1–31. S. M. Baugh concludes,

> Instead, the simple meaning here and elsewhere in Hebrews is to attest solemnly to the reality or truth of something: "to attest, testify, bear witness."[9]

Allowing Baugh's conclusion to influence our understanding of Hebrews 11:2, taken with the relationship between Hebrews 11:1 and 11:2 (as indicated by the connecting word *gar* (γάρ = "for" [gives the reason for verse 1]), we conclude that the reason faith is objective fact is because God's testimony (wisdom) stands in back of it. The Old Testament saints believed the promised future events would come, but their faith itself rested upon divine testimony of these things. A less stringent paraphrase can be: "For in connection with their faith God testified [about what would happen in the future] to the saints of old."[10]

The author of Hebrews illustrates this very point when he discusses the unbelieving recipients of God's Word during the Exodus. They failed to mix the truth they heard with faith and therefore failed to enter into God's rest (during the Exodus when God promised to supply all of their needs up to and including reaching the land of promise or the future temporal [millennial] kingdom under God's direct rule on earth). In contrast, those who *did* believe the testimony of God about their earthly future and caught a full view of the substance of God's kingdom promise and its ramifications, by faith, rested during their wilderness journey. As God directed, shaded, heated, fed, and protected them on their way to the land of promise, the faithful enjoyed the journey and left the "driving" to God. These faithful "resters" will enjoy the temporal kingdom, as well. This is what the author of Hebrews calls "God's rest."

Therefore, the typical idea that these people simply had a mental image of their possible future that motivated them to act in faith towards God's promise misses the point. They had more than a mere mental image. They had tangible evidence because the promises of God transform faith. They had hard evidence of their future drawn from what God promised and delivered during their journey.

A New Way of Thinking About Faith

To set up our conclusion that Hebrews 11 expands upon the saints recorded in the Old Testament as simultaneous participants in and witnesses to the coming temporal kingdom of God by faith, we will look at some supporting exegetical details, followed by an interpretation of Hebrews 11:1-31 that illustrates and defends this conclusion.

Our thesis requires that Hebrews 11:1 not be a lexical definition of faith, but a contextual characterization of a key aspect of the faith of the Old Testament witnesses. This is a very important point. In our judgment, it holds the key to understanding what kind of faith is necessary to successfully live the Christian life in general and to survive the persecution of Satan and his Antichrist in particular. Absent this view, many will continue to believe that to live a successful Christian life, it is necessary to have a faith that very few can understand or obtain.

Stop chasing the foolish notions taught by many that faith is an elusive lucky charm that forces God to act on our behalf. The fact that faith in Hebrews 11 is a contextual characterization and not a dictionary definition better explains the call of the author for his readers to utilize the "witness" of the Old Testament saints. S.M Baugh summaries:

A characterization does not give an exhaustive or abstract definition of something, but brings out certain key features or even distinguishing outcomes of something. For example: "Pure and undefiled religion before God the Father is this: to care for orphans and widows in their misfortune and to keep oneself unstained by the world" (James 1:27; ESV). The care for needy persons and the avoidance of sin do not *define* "pure and undefiled religion," but they do well *characterize* piety in action. The word "faith" is treated the same way in Hebrews 11; the author presents faith in action, as comes out so clearly by his repeated use of the instrumental dative πίστει ("by faith") 18 times in the 40 verses of this chapter.[11]

The author of Hebrews treats the persevering faith of the Old Testament saints as they now testify to us as a "cloud of witnesses" (Heb. 12:1). Misunderstanding this peculiarity has led to support for the skewed interpretation of the terms mentioned above, as well as to the failure to appreciate key details in the appraisals of the Old Testament saints depicted in Hebrews 11:1-31. The writer focuses our attention on the faith of the Old Testament examples that apprehended the promised yet unseen future outcome of human history as we know it through divine testimony. It is this faith that provided the basis for their courageous walks of integrity, often in the face of intense persecution. Their faith acted!

This is the exact behavior necessary on the part of those sovereignly chosen to face the Great Persecution. That generation of faithful followers of Jesus Christ must apprehend the promised, unseen future outcome of human history as we know it through the record of God's divine testimony (Matthew 24-25). Then, it must persevere in this faith. If you truly believe what God promises will happen, then those things will be just as real to you now as the events themselves will be when they happen. Faith puts an equal sign between the promise and its fulfillment. One is just as concrete as the other because God is the author of both. In essence, if God says it is going to rain today, faith makes one take his raincoat and umbrella in the morning.

Faith that what God said will happen must provide us with the courage to stand and face whatever God allows to be each of our specific destinies. Since we know what the behavior of Satan and his Antichrist will be, all that is left is for us to do is to prepare to look intently into the face of Almighty God as we march into that destiny. Do you have the courage?

The Saints of Old Yet Speaks to Us

As stated, the faith of the Old Testament saints rested upon God's promises spoken to them as solemn testimony by the one whose Word always comes with a pledge of complete dependability. Because of this fact, the saints who received prior revelation and responded with faith have themselves become "a cloud of witnesses" (Heb. 12:1) to us.[12] Look at the goodness of God! We are so blessed not only to have God's promises, but to have the testimonies of men and women who took those promises seriously.

It is clear that the author of Hebrews does not refer to these individuals as examples for us to emulate, although that may be a less important inference of our text. Rather, he refers to them first and foremost as witnesses who confirm the veracity of the heavenly truths that God promised them. Some have erred by understanding "witness" in the phrase "cloud of witnesses" to mean that these inscripturated saints are mere spectators who watch us as we run our race (Heb. 12:1), rather than fellow travelers on the same road who are posting road marks of encouragement for us as we march behind them.

In this regards, S. M. Baugh argues,

> The word "witness" (μάρτυς) does imply some sort of personal experience of an event or person, but in Greek, *martus* includes the notion that the person attests or bears witness in some sense to what he has seen. The notion of acting as an onlooker is normally communicated in Greek with the noun ὁ θεατής ("spectator," "onlooker"; not used in the Bible) or forms of the verbs θεωρέω or θεάομαι rather than with μάρτυς or its word group.[13]

The saints of Hebrews 11:4–40 stand as witnesses to us of the end of this world as we know it (God wins) and the benefits of entrusting ourselves to God's sovereign outworking of His perfect plan in this age in order to set up His kingdom for the next. Scripture not only tells us that God wins, but how He wins and what awaits those who trust in Him. Specifically how they speak to us and what each says to us is the goal of our examination of each witness in this chapter.

Therefore, we should see in the witness of the Old Testament saints the evidence necessary to continue walking with God in the midst of our present situation, even when we cannot see how its specific end will play out. The Old Testament saints are not mere spectators of our race, but cheerleaders and teammates who champion us as we run. They are the proof that we are not running in vain. They serve as our rock solid unambiguous evidence upon which we are to act.

This interpretation of Hebrews 11 gives us insight into the whole epistle to the Hebrews, as well as how we are to understand the consummation of all things and our approach to it. Hebrews 11 shows that the writer regards the entire Old Testament record as capable of witnessing to the end-times events introduced by Christ. Just as James instructs, the faithful need only ask God for wisdom. The Old Testament illustrates the process and the outcomes of living by the wisdom obtained from God. Once wisdom is obtained, God fully expects us to continue in faithfulness. The author of

Hebrews presents several detailed case studies for just how this process works, which can serve as a roadmap through the Great Persecution of Satan and his Antichrist.

Testimony Time

In light of this understanding of Hebrews 11:1-2, we can now turn our attention to the Old Testament witnesses presented in Hebrews 11. To regard these witnesses as "heroes of faith" who illustrate an abstract definition of faith is to misunderstand their function as witnesses to God's coming kingdom and the blessings it holds for both national Israel and the Church. Even a cursory reading of the original records of these witnesses in the Old Testament reveals that they are not the best representatives of faithfulness.

In this context, the examples chosen from the scriptural testimony support and illustrate the conduct of God's people the author hopes will encourage his readers to abandon any attempt to apostatize from Christ. In the heat of battle, we must remain with Christ. This is a point we intend to make concerning that generation of believers chosen by God to face the unparalleled persecution of Satan and his Antichrist. To abandon Christ will leave one without hope and guarantee the undesirable outcome—physical death in shame—which is the very thing he or she intended to escape.

Abel: Your Best Pleases God

Abel, the second son of Adam and Eve, is the first witness of the Old Testament saints to offer evidence for faithfulness in Hebrews 11. Verse 4 begins: "By faith Abel offered God a greater sacrifice than Cain."

"Greater" renders the Greek noun *pleiōn* (πλείων) here. The term does not communicate the intended meaning of the text. The author uses a rare meaning of *polus/pleiōn*, which denotes something of *more value* or *importance*. This sense is reflected in the NIV's translation of Matthew 6:25: "Is not life *more important* [πλεῖον] than food and the body *more important* than clothes?" (emphasis added).

Since all Old Testament sacrifices were mere shadows of the ultimate sacrifice of the Lord Jesus, we know that Abel's sacrifice was "greater" in a way only human effort could attain. Although we are not told in the text that God provided instructions for the sacrifice, we can deduct that God provided them, since Cain's sacrifice was rejected.

Cain's sacrifice did not demonstrate a commitment to the seriousness of God's ultimate sacrifice for mankind. The seriousness of sin demanded a sacrifice that only God could give. In symbolic foreshadowing of God's ultimate gift, both Cain and Abel were instructed to give their best to God. This could only be attained by the death of an animal, not fruits and vegetables. In giving the Levitical law, God had Moses record what most likely was already known — that only the death of an animal was sufficient to atone for sin. Therefore, Cain's sacrifice failed because it was inappropriate. It did not meet the standard for the atonement of sin. (Later, we learn that fruit and vegetables were sufficient only for guilt offerings and not for the atonement.)

Abel's sacrifice in Hebrews 11:4, then, can only be regarded as greater than that of Cain because, as the text says, through faith he received divine testimony to his righteousness at the offering of his gifts. It is at this juncture that rendering *martureō* as "to commend" or "to approve" misses the author's real point in verse 4.[14] Rather, the sense of the text is that God offered commentary on the sacrifices of the two boys. In essence, God told them who passed and who failed. Instead of receiving God's wisdom and meeting God's requirements the rest of his natural life, Cain abandoned righteousness for evil. Consequently, the text gives no report concerning Cain's sacrifices after this.

The power and importance of Abel's example did not end with his physical death. The writer of Hebrews informs us that Abel's voice can still be heard. S. M. Baugh captures the sense of Hebrews 11:4 when he writes,

> Now comes a most instructive phrase in Hebrews' treatment of Abel. The author clearly alludes in the last clause of Heb. 11:4 to Gen. 4:10 when he observes that Abel

speaks in death. But there is a significant difference. In Gen. 4:10 Abel's blood cries out to God from the earth—surely as a cry for vengeance against his murderer which God duly executes by pronouncing judgment on Cain. . . But in Heb. 11:4, Abel himself speaks *to us* through faith even though he is dead. The author's point is perfectly clear. Once the cry of Abel's blood to God was recorded as part of the living and active voice of Scripture (Heb. 4:12), Abel became a living witness who "speaks" to us of the righteousness of faith (cf. Heb. 11:7).

A look back at the Genesis account of Abel's deed reveals the act before God's characterization of it. In other words, God expressed pleasure with Abel's offering only after Abel brought it. We are not told how Abel knew what to do, but God confirmed His choice. Abel did the right thing to please God and was rewarded verbally. The object of Abel's faith was that to which his sacrifice pointed and the blood (Jesus Christ and His sacrifice for the sins of mankind) that speaks better than his own (Heb. 12:24). Just imagine Abel either running along beside us or planting roadside banners waving in the wind that read: "Your best pleases God."

By respecting God's wishes, Abel testified to God's ultimate plan by bringing his best as an offering to God. This imitates God, who gave His best for us. Our faith must take Abel's testimony as evidence of God's faithfulness if we are chosen to be that generation to face the persecution of Satan and his Antichrist. Abel is proof that giving God our best brings divine favor. It may not keep us from experiencing physical death, but the rewards God has promised after death (resurrection, public praise, and authority to rule in God's kingdom) are assured.

Abel's testimony is hard evidence that, if called upon to make a choice between the perfect will of God (potentially, physical death at the hand of Antichrist) and the permissive will of God (potentially, surviving the Great Persecution by aggressively seeking avenues to survive), we will walk by faith and give God our best, knowing full well that God gave His very best at Calvary. What Abel saw in the future, we see in the past. What remains is this question: Will we give God our best if called to do so during the end times?

Enoch: Translation Without Death

From Abel, the author of Hebrews moves to the testimony of Enoch. The account in Genesis 5:18–24 reports that Enoch "walked with God," then "he was not, for God took him." The LXX translates the Hebrew that stands in back of the phrase "walking with God" in Genesis 5:22, 24 and elsewhere as "pleasing" God. This is a true rendering of the Hebrew.

There are two things to focus on in Hebrews 11:5 and 6 that advance our thesis that Hebrews 11 is a second source of evidence or proof that God is faithful to His promises. First, following his theme regarding faith in this chapter, the author asserts that it was by faith (πίστει) that Enoch was "removed" and "not found" "so that he would not see death." Secondly, the writer once more underscores that divine testimony is foundational to Enoch's faith, with the result that Enoch could join the "cloud of witnesses." S. M. Baugh adds,

> The focus of attention at the beginning of v. 5 is upon God's translation of Enoch as the eventual outcome of his faith: "By faith Enoch was taken up so that he should not see death, and he was not found, because God had taken him" (ESV). The repetition here should not be missed: "Enoch was taken up. . . he should not see death. . . he was not found. . . God had taken him."[15]

This emphasis is clearly with an eye upon that generation of faithful followers of Jesus Christ who hope to escape death by their own translation (e.g., 1 Thess. 4:16). Enoch had the same faith as ours. Consequently, the outcome for us is potentially the same, as well.

Enoch received testimony that he pleased God. This is an essential element in the Hebrew writer's revelation of Enoch's faith. He wrote: "Before his removal he had been commended as having pleased God." The NET Bible's decision to translate the Greek verb *mamarturatai* (μεμαρτύρηται) with the infinitive as "he has been commended as having pleased God" does not follow Greek usage for this verb. The *New American Standard Bible* makes the text explicitly clear that Enoch himself "obtained the *witness*. . . that. . . he was pleasing to God" (emphasis added).

Moses does not tell us in the Genesis account how it is that Enoch received this witness or testimony, or when during his life that he got the report, but he says that "Enoch pleased [or 'walked with'] God" in Genesis 5:22, 24. It is logical to conclude that Enoch would have known this himself and therefore would have concluded that God's report gave him evidence for the reality of all the other things for which he hoped. After all, Genesis 5:22 says that Enoch walked with God for three hundred years and, thus, his walk entailed a lifetime of close communion with the Lord. Hence, Enoch's faith rested firmly on divine testimony.

The nature of that testimony is discernable in the report of Jude 14–15:

> Now Enoch, the seventh in descent beginning with Adam, even prophesied of them, saying, "Look! The Lord is coming with thousands and thousands of his holy ones, to execute judgment on all, and to convict every person of all their thoroughly ungodly deeds that they have committed, and all the harsh words that ungodly sinners have spoken against him."

Jude makes it clear that Enoch knew a lot more than we are told. After all, three hundred years is a long time to walk with God. God must have shared with Enoch much insight about the judgment that was to come. Clearly, Enoch knew of the cleansing of the earth that would immediately precede God's physical descent to earth.[16] At minimum, he knew that the angels would be involved in the process.

Enoch runs alongside of us as we run waving the banner that reads: "Translation without death is possible." We have both the promise of God's Word through Enoch's typological pattern fulfillment and Paul's promise that God can and will translate His people out of this world. Enoch's life is clearly evidence for our faith.

Noah: God Delivers the Righteous Before His Wrath Falls on the Wicked

The third recipient of praise from the author of Hebrews is Noah. Noah is a witness to the reality of God's faithfulness when man acts by faith and God responds to it. As evidenced by other passages in the New Testament, Noah's story of deliverance is an ideal typological pattern that illustrates that God delivers the righteous before His wrath falls on the wicked.

The author informs us that Noah received divine warning (i.e., testimony) "about things not yet seen." These unseen things were so designated because they had not yet happened. Likewise, other Old Testament saints apprehended future events, as in the example of Joseph and the Exodus (v. 22). The author indicates this happened by faith, though it was "from afar" (v. 13). We, too, do not perceive the full consummation of future events (Heb. 2:8), but we do see them moving toward fulfillment in the coming of the Lord Jesus (Heb. 2:9; cf. Heb. 1:1–3; 9:28). Faith, then, gives us sight like that of the servant of Elisha (2 Kings 6:15–17). That's why it was in *reverent faith* upon which Noah acted after hearing the divine warning of coming judgment by building the ark, declares our author.

Since Noah set out to build the ark one hundred twenty years before it rained, some might conclude that Noah was operating on mere shadows of possibilities. At this point, S. M. Baugh is insightful when he writes,

> We must distinguish what was just said about Noah's faith as one which apprehended future events from a common interpretation of Heb. 11 that believers somehow *create* these realities in their minds. . . Hebrews is not interested in merely psychological phenomenon. The reality is in the historical events as they occur, but the proof of their fulfillment in history is the giving of divine testimony, in this case when Noah was "warned" of future events.[17]

It is possible that God allowed Noah to fall into a sleep during which he saw the events unfold.

However, no such indication is given in the Bible. We are told that God warned Noah, and upon that basis, Noah acted.

In Hebrews 11:7, the author communicates that Noah's preparation of the ark resulted in the rescue of his household. This resulted in the condemnation of the world through faith. These interrelated points are most instructive for our author's understanding of the consummation of all things. Specifically, it raises the issues of typological fulfillment.

When Hebrews mentions that Noah's acts of faith resulted in the salvation of his house, there is an echo of a typological pattern that is repeated throughout the Scriptures — of Moses and the Exodus, of Jesus and His house from sin, and of Jesus and His Church from the Great Persecution, even if that deliverance does not necessarily look the way many people expect. Thus, Noah, the savior of his house, is suggestively presented as a type of Christ, the Savior of God's household. Likewise, the rescue of God's people in Noah's day is accompanied by the annihilation of all life by divine wrath.

At the end of Hebrews 11:7, the author focuses upon Noah's becoming an heir of that righteousness, which is "according to faith." S. M. Baugh concludes,

> This is a remarkable point, particularly since Noah's righteousness is stressed in the Genesis narrative: "Noah was a righteous

man, blameless in his generation. Noah walked with God. . . 'Go into the ark, you and all your household, for I have seen you are righteous before me in this generation'" (Gen. 6:9; 7:1; ESV; cf. Ezek. 14:14, 20; 2 Pet. 2:5). . . Hebrews was aware of this stress, and he himself also stresses Noah's righteousness. But the statement on Noah's righteousness in Hebrews represents a critical interpretative development made in one masterful stroke.[18]

Noah is our witness that righteousness is rewarded with deliverance in the face of unparalleled destruction. Noah waves a banner that reads: "God delivers the righteous before His wrath falls on the wicked." The evidence that God will deliver His people before His wrath falls is clearly seen in Noah and the great flood. Since "faith is the evidence of things not seen," the Scriptures give us the promise of God (1 Thess. 4:16) and the witness of Noah, which provide ample evidence. We can persevere because we have the facts.

Abraham: Resurrection From the Dead

In any list of the significant warriors of the Old Testament, one would naturally expect Abraham to appear. Abraham and his seed provide a rich background for teaching several critical truths necessary to stand the test of Satan and his Antichrist at the eschatological end.

To begin, the author of Hebrews portrays Abraham, Isaac, and Jacob as fellow heirs of the same promise. They were pilgrims, primarily because they experienced the land, but never built a permanent city. This wandering was necessary because their inheritance did not include elements of this world alone, but heavenly elements that required divine assets to possess. Equally, if Abraham took God's words literally, a significant amount of time was necessary in order to see fulfillment. The combining of earthly and heavenly elements can only come after the final resurrection of all those who have direct association with the promised inheritance.

When called to leave his country, kindred, and father's house, Abraham went out in ignorance of many details concerning how and when God would fulfill the making of a great nation, the making of a great name, and the making of him into a great blessing to others. In his lifetime, he saw the beginnings of God's fulfillment. Abraham "sojourned in the land God promises to give to his descendents." He begin nation-building with a special son, Isaac, and saw others greatly benefit from an association with himself. However, he only saw the beginnings of these promises.

In other words, in unfolding the revelation that the promise would include more than just what Abraham could experience during his physical lifetime, God withheld the final *experience* of ownership of the Canaanite real estate. It forced Abraham to meditate on the complete fulfillment of the covenant (Gen. 12:1-4, land, nation, blessings) and the necessity of a future resurrection after which he would experience the final fulfillment.

There are two reasons God withheld the final phase of the fulfillment of Abraham's earthly inheritance. First, Abraham needed to look in faith for a greater city "whose designer and builder is God," where he and God would live together; second, that Abraham and his fellow heirs would not have this inheritance apart from all of those to whom God intended the promise (Heb. 11:40). National Israel must altogether inherit the "enduring" heavenly city (Heb. 13:14).

We can rejoice that Abraham, by faith, did see the heavenly city, although for Abraham and the patriarchs, the view was "from afar" (Heb. 11:13-14; cf. v. 27). The distance of viewpoint was not because Abraham's faith was weak. Just the opposite! It was because Abraham initiated the promise and must wait until the promised kings and nations (numbering as the stars) also find fulfillment.

God could easily have given Abraham and "barren Sarah" (v. 11) a natural son early in life, but He waited until it became clear that the birth of the child was a complete and total work of God. Then, after Isaac was born and the promise was explicitly fulfilled, He commanded Abraham to offer up Isaac as a sacrifice. The purpose of this command was to teach Abraham that God is able to raise the dead, which Abraham rightly concluded and did receive Isaac in resurrection, if we speak symbolically (Heb. 11:19). S. M. Baugh concludes,

In the way the author of Hebrews interprets these patriarchal narratives, we see that he regards not only God's words as oracular but the events recorded in Scripture as revelatory as well—they all "speak" as it were. By word, God testified to Abraham of a future inheritance and of natural descendants by repeating His promises and sealing them with an oath-bound eternal covenant (Gen. 15, 17). By event, God held off the fulfillment, so that Abraham and his heirs were led, in time, "to long for a better [homeland], that is a heavenly one. . . which God prepared" (Heb. 11:16). Therefore even the events of Abraham's life were directed by God to be revelatory.[19]

As we face the possibility of being that unique generation to face the Great Persecution of Satan and his Antichrist, we must look to words and deeds of past saints who face stressful times and copy their behavior. The promise of resurrection and rule with Christ in His kingdom awaits us if we do.

As they run alongside of us, Abraham and his immediate heirs are holding up banners that read: "Resurrection from the dead," "A heavenly city comes down to earth," and "Possible death before final inheritance." These testimonies give ample evidence for our faith to persevere even in the face of death. Regardless of the temporal outcome of the

Great Persecution, God will win and so will we. The only question left unanswered concerns out enjoyment of God's temporal kingdom. If we are faith, we will enjoy. If we are not faithful — well let's focus on being faithful!

Exodus: God's Miraculous Deliverance

Hebrews 11:23-31 focuses on the Exodus and entrance into the land of Israel. It is not a surprise that the author of Hebrews would spend time on this great event. As the central typological pattern or picture of God's special work to bring His elect out of slavery, both spiritual and physical, the Exodus warrants special attention. The author of Hebrews picks Moses to receive the lion's share of the attention because his story fills in the importance of this section for New Testament believers.

Yet, it is the Exodus event itself that holds the most importance. The reason being that the Exodus was God's first historical deliverance of his elect out of the midst of a hostile environment (Egypt). The second great example is our Lord's deliverance of God's elect out of the midst of a hostile environment (sin). The third and final great deliverance of God will be the removal of his people (the Church and National Israel) out of a hostile environment (the Great Persecution). In as much the first two events are completed facts, we must allow them to serve as evidence of

God's faithfulness regarding the third and final great deliverance.

Moses' Parents: the Providence of God

The Scriptures inform us that "By faith, when Moses was born, his parents hid him for three months." How was the act of hiding the child the product of faith? In our case, what oath-bound communication of God became the evidence upon which Amram and Jochebed acted? The text gives two reasons for their actions: (1) because they saw the child was beautiful and (2) because they were not afraid of the edict of the king of Egypt.

Perhaps the reason Amram and Jochebed were not afraid of the king's edict is because God had ably demonstrated the ease with which His people could get around it. Historically, we know the circumstances that surrounded the birth of Moses. During this particular time, all newborn Hebrew males were to be put to death. In this atmosphere and at this remarkable time in history, the baby Moses was born.

The book of Exodus begins with an explanation of the remarkable growth in numbers of the sons of Israel from a mere seventy individuals to numbers "more numerous and stronger" than their Egyptian host (Exodus 1:9). To deal with this exploding population, the king of Egypt began a program to control the Israelite population. The Egyptians oppressed the people with hard labor. However, their efforts produced the opposite result. The text states that "the more the Egyptians oppressed them, the more they multiplied and spread" (Exodus 1:12).

The failed policy was replaced with infanticide. The king of Egypt ordered the Hebrew midwives to kill all male babies born to Israelite women. How long this practice was to continue is not explicitly indicated. However, the policy never got off the ground because the two Hebrew midwives (Shiphrah and Puah) charged with implementing it refused to obey the king. Ostensibly because they "feared God" (Exodus 1:17), the Scriptures add. When challenged about their conduct, the midwives reported to the king that the Israelite women had babies faster than they could keep up. Exodus 1:20–21 report that God blessed the midwives greatly because of their actions. The first chapter of Exodus concludes with the king subsequently placing the responsibility for the murder of newborn boys in hands of the Egyptian people. Pharaoh commanded all his people to throw newborn boys into the river. It is under this last attempt that Moses was born.

How aggressive the Egyptian people were in obeying their king is not stated. However, given the beginning of the second chapter of Exodus, the threat was viable and well known. In what is clearly one of the most impressive cases of irony, Moses would be saved by both the Egyptian king and the river.

We are told that at the birth of Moses, his parents hid the child for three months. The author of Hebrews indicates one reason they did so was because they were not afraid of the king's edict. The text does not indicate a direct link between the parents of Moses and the midwives, but it is logical that they were aware of the king's policies and God's deliverance of the Israelite children by the midwives. Since God had thwarted Pharaoh's edict in the past, there was every expectation that He would do it again. God's conduct was ample evidence that faith would preserve the lives of the Israelites' male children.

Upon his birth, Moses' parents discerned a second reason to hide their baby boy — the providence of God. The basis of their discernment was the beauty or goodness of the child. The New Testament correctly reflects the sense of the Old Testament with the translation "because they saw the child was beautiful" (Exodus 2:2). The term is variously translated "when she saw that he was a 'healthy child'" (NET), "fine child" (ESV, NIV), "goodly child" (KJV, RSV), and "beautiful" (NASB), which are all different ways of catching the sense of the text. The same Greek word found in Hebrews 11 as a description of Moses also occurs in Acts 7:20. The repeated emphasis on this aspect of Moses' life suggests something beyond the ordinary.

The original Hebrew term is *tov* (טוֹב). It occurs in Genesis 1 as a commentary on God's acts of creation and signifies whatever enhances, promotes, produces, or is conducive for life. Was this the attitude of Moses' parents as they beheld the face of their newborn child?

While every mother sees her newly born child as beautiful and special, are we to detect theological significance from the words of Moses' parents? The author of Hebrews continues his emphasis on both word and event as instruments that communicate God's will and form the basis for an active faith. In the case of Moses' parents, that the child was born "beautiful" seemed to signal a divine intent that could not possibly find fulfillment in death so soon after birth. Their confidence in God's sovereign hand warranted their actions.

Moses: God Can Deliver His People Out of a Hostile Nation

At the center of the author's presentation of the Exodus is Moses. The text does not explain any events connected with his life after being discovered by Pharaoh's daughter. Those thirty-plus years are left in silence. However, with his unique rescue from Pharaoh's edict and his own mother's instrumental role in his upbringing, it is difficult to believe that he and his blood relatives did not discern some significance from those events, in addition to the fact that the Hebrews had been in Egypt just over three hundred years. The loud voice of Joseph's bones proclaiming the promise that God would return His children to their homeland after four generations (four hundred years) must have had some part in the education of this special Hebrew boy.

The author of Hebrews resumes his account of the life of Moses with the statement that "Moses refused to be called the son of Pharaoh's daughter, choosing rather to be ill-treated with the people of God than to enjoy sin's fleeting pleasure." The author of Hebrews then explains, "He [Moses] regarded abuse suffered for Christ to be greater wealth than the treasures of Egypt, for his eyes were fixed on the reward."

One author explains the sense of Moses' actions. He writes,

> In [Hebrews] 11:26 we read that Moses preferred *the reproach of Christ* to the treasures of Egypt. This phrase, *the reproach of Christ,* is explained by its usage in 13:13, "Let us therefore go forth unto him without the camp, bearing his reproach." This reproach is thus seen to be a reproach which Christ Himself first bore and which we now bear together with Him. So we must similarly interpret the reproach of Christ borne by Moses. This does not imply that Moses had a prophetic knowledge of the sufferings of the future Messiah, but rather that the reproach which Moses bore was objectively identical with the reproach suffered by Christ and His people throughout the ages. This implies, therefore, that in back of all the reproaches and sufferings which God's people have endured stood Christ.[20]

The author utilizes several key phrases to describe the events surrounding the life of Moses that appear rather unusual. In what sense did Moses know about events connected with Christ? What was the reward upon which Moses fixed his eyes? At what point did Moses become conscious of God's will for his life? Prior to fleeing Egypt, did Moses have personal knowledge of God? These are important questions in light of the tone and position the author of Hebrews takes about him.

In Hebrews, the quick rehearsal of Moses' providential deliverance from the edict of Pharaoh gives way to a more detailed interpretation of his acts of faith. The author reports that Moses' first act of faith was his rejection of his status as a member of Pharaoh's family. The exact circumstances of this event are not detailed. His position in Pharaoh's court contrasts with the ill treatment of the people of God. It is clear that the author of Hebrews is offering commentary on the life of Moses and not the specifics that led him to make such a choice.

However, the author of Hebrews insists that the motivation for Moses' actions was his knowledge that he was a member of "the people of God." Being raised by his mother in the home of Pharaoh's daughter gave Moses a choice: the wealth of Egypt or the ill treatment of God's people. We can only suppose that Moses was educated about his roots by his mother. God's promises and miraculous deeds in the lives of Abraham, Isaac, Jacob, and Joseph must have caused Moses to see the futility of Egyptian's kingdom and the ultimate success of the promised kingdom of the Hebrews.

The significance of Moses' choice is further clarified as a choice between the wealth of Egypt and the reward of God earned through suffering with Christ.

With the events of Christ's life fresh in his mind, the New Testament writer sees the events resulting from Moses' choices as parallel to the suffering that all believers endure for Christ. The goal or motivation of Moses' conduct was "the reward," a reward Moses knew about and so motivated him that he abandoned the comforts of Egypt for it. The obvious questions are these: How did Moses know about the reward and what was it?

It is difficult to know the precise period during the life of Moses that he came to have this commitment. It would appear that he had these convictions before he left Egypt the first time. This would necessitate Moses having knowledge prior to leaving Egypt for his forty-year sojourn in the wilderness.

"His eyes were fixed on the reward" is the unique way the writer of Hebrews expresses Moses' motivation. Literally, the Greek suggests, "Because he was looking ahead to the reward. . ." We believe this is the proper translation of the critical clause and suggests that repeated concentrated attention is given the matter. Moses set his sights on the reward of God. While we are not able to detail the specifics of Moses' knowledge, we know that the eschatological reward is the full inheritance (rest) repeatedly rehearsed throughout the book of Hebrews. Ultimately, it is a share in the glory of Christ at God's right hand specifically identified in Hebrews 12:1–2. Such conviction inspired behavior that only God can give. It is the reality of God that drove Moses once he left Egypt the first time. Again, the writer of Hebrews states the motivation of Moses' actions. The NET Bible translates the text, "He persevered as though he could see the one who is invisible." Scholars do not agree whether the emphasis of the verse is (1) that Moses really did see the invisible God or (2) that he persevered as one who did see Him. If we maintain the apparent chronological order of the text, we must conclude that the writer is referring to an event prior to Moses leaving Egypt the first time to sojourn in the land of Midian.[21] The Old Testament text does not indicate any explicit contact between Moses and God prior to this time, but it does make clear that Moses held a faith that had both substance and evidence "of things not seen." Who or what informed Moses we do not know, but the clarity of his sight once informed is compelling.

Upon returning to Egypt after experiencing God on the mountain, Moses continued to operate by faith. He allowed the blood of a lamb to protect him from the angel of death. Exodus 12:1–30 makes clear that God informed Moses about the Passover event and gave clear instructions about what was to be done.

Highlighting the events of the Exodus, the author of Hebrews summarizes the exit of the children of Israel from the land of Egypt by focusing on the crossing of the Red Sea (the last obstacle upon leaving Egypt) and the fall of Jericho (the first major obstacle to entering the land). Both events were the direct result of God's sovereign intervention. The Exodus narration concludes with a mention of the prostitute Rahab, who recognized the power of the victorious march of the Hebrews and chose to identify with them. Her knowledge of the history of the Hebrews since leaving Egypt caused her to conclude that the God of the Jews was true and worthy of worship.

The events and primary participants of the Exodus allow the author of Hebrews to make a compelling case for acting in faith. If faith is the evidence of things not seen and is ultimately informed by the testimony of God, the Exodus is powerful evidence of God's faithfulness to deliver His people out of the power of another nation.

The author of Hebrews concludes his characterization of faith by presenting an abbreviated laundry list of Old Testament saints who had victory over the enemies of God. Some are specifically named and others are identified by action. He summarizes:

> And what more shall I say? For time will fail me if I tell of Gideon, Barak, Samson, Jephthah, of David and Samuel and the prophets. Through faith they conquered

kingdoms, administered justice, gained what was promised, shut the mouths of lions, quenched raging fire, escaped the edge of the sword, gained strength in weakness, became mighty in battle, put foreign armies to flight, and women received back their dead raised to life. But others were tortured, not accepting release, to obtain resurrection to a better life.

And others experienced mocking and flogging, and even chains and imprisonment. They were stoned, sawed apart, murdered with the sword; they went about in sheepskins and goatskins; they were destitute, afflicted, ill-treated (the world was not worthy of them); they wandered in deserts and mountains and caves and openings in the earth. And these all were commended for their faith, yet they did not receive what was promised. For God had provided something better for us, so that they would be made perfect together with us.

Conclusion

In conclusion, we have seen that Hebrews 11 presents the Old Testament saints as witnesses who point to those unseen, hoped-for realities that have been brought to definitive, inaugurated clarity by Christ. The future kingdom of God is a central theme of the book of Hebrews. The author does not think this inappropriate, for he sees it as the main (although evolving) focal point of the Old Testament Scriptures. The Old Testament saints reviewed in Hebrews 11 are presented as witnesses to various aspects of the kingdom of God, which Christ highlighted for us during His earthly ministry.

The author's presentation of the Old Testament saints as witnesses to the ultimate historical realities makes his case in the Epistle to the Hebrews quite strongly. Given that his audience intended to center its hope on the Mosaic system, our author invokes the Old Testament saints themselves as witnesses to an exclusive faith in the new covenant Mediator, Jesus—*not* faith in the "weak and useless" (Heb. 7:18) shadowy types "of the good things to come" (Heb. 10:1; cf. 9:11). To return to the Mosaic Law after Christ is to trample Him under foot (Heb. 10:29) and abandon the faith of the Old Testament saints themselves. For "many prophets and righteous men" saw these things "from afar" and longed to see them (as do we), but they did not (Matt. 13:17; cf., e.g., John 1:45; 8:56; 12:39–41; 1 Pet. 1:10; Heb. 11:13).

The author of Hebrews is essentially reiterating what Jesus said to the Jews who had "put their trust in Moses" (John 5:45) at the same time they plotted to kill him (John 5:18). "If you believed Moses," Jesus said, "you would believe me; *because he wrote about me.* But if you do not believe what Moses wrote, how will you believe my words?" (John 5:46–47, emphasis added). Moses himself had

Faith: A Characterization

considered "the reproach of Christ to be greater wealth than the treasures of Egypt" (Heb. 11:26), but his descendants preferred the empty rites of Levitical ceremony in place of that sacrifice of Christ to which Levi and Aaron pointed and in which they, themselves, had put their faith. Levi, Moses, Aaron, and all the Old Testament saints are witnesses to Christ by their confession of faith and the events of their lives under God's sovereign direction in both revelatory word and deed. These simple truths are sufficient to sustain us if we are but willing to run the race set before us.

---

[1] *Faith and Mission* Vol. 12, vnp.12.1.82–12.1.83 (Southeastern Baptist Theological Seminary, 1995; 2005).

[2] Gerald L. Borchert, "A Superior Book: Hebrews," *RevExp* 82 (Summer 1985), 381.

[3] Paul Ellingworth, *The Epistle to the Hebrews: A Commentary on the Greek Text* (Grand Rapids, Mich.; Carlisle [England: W.B. Eerdmans; Paternoster Press, 1993), 564.

[4] "The Cloud of Witnesses in Hebrews 11," S. M. Baugh, *WTJ* 68 (Spring 2006) *Westminster Theological Journal Vol. 68*, vnp.68.1.113 (Westminster Theological Seminary, 2006; 2007).

[5] Ibid., 116.

[6] Horst Robert Balz and Gerhard Schneider, *Exegetical Dictionary of the New Testament*, translation of: *Exegetisches Worterbuch zum Neuen Testament*, 3:407 (Grand Rapids, Mich.: Eerdmans, 1990–c1993).

[7] Baugh, "The Cloud of Witnesses in Hebrews 11," 115.

[8] Ibid., 115. Three of which he uses in his epistle: *parrāsia* (3:6; 4:16; 10:19, 35); *kauchāma* (3:6); and *plārophoria* (6:11; 10:22).

[9] Baugh, 118.

[10] Baugh, "The Cloud of Witnesses in Hebrews 11," (footnote 24) writes,

The passive ἐμαρτυρήθησαν has God as the implied subject—so also with passive μαρτυρέω in Heb. 7:8, 17; 11:5, 39; and with other verbs elsewhere (e.g., future passive λαληθησομένων in 3:5, "things to be spoken," may be paraphrased: "things which God would later reveal"; or ἐλαλήθη in 11:8, where the reference is to God's promise to Abraham), cf. Daniel Wallace, *Greek Grammar Beyond the Basics* (Grand Rapids: Zondervan, 1996), 437–38. The active genitive absolute statement in 11:4 confirms this interpretation: μαρτυροῦντος ... τοῦ θεοῦ, "God bearing witness." The ἐν in the phrase ἐν ταῦτη communicates a general specification, "in connection with" (cf. BDAG, ἐν meaning #12). The author avoids the often repeated dative πίστει because he does not want to communicate an instrumental idea here, contra Attridge, *Hebrews,* 314 and n. 104.

[11] Baugh, 119.

[12] "The metaphor of the 'cloud' of witnesses refers to 'a compact, numberless throng' (BDAG) or a 'host,' and was so used elsewhere in Greek literature; cf. Bruce, *Hebrews,* 333 n. 7. The strong inferential conjunction τοιγαροῦν ('consequently, then. . .'), which introduces Heb. 12:1 identifies the host of witnesses here as the various OT saints of 11:4–40; cf. N. Clayton Croy, *Endurance in Suffering: Hebrews 12:1–13 in Its Rhetorical, Religious, and Philosophical Context* (SNTSMS 98; Cambridge: Cambridge University Press, 1998).

[13] Baugh defends his conclusion with the following comments:

> See, e.g., John 2:23; Acts 4:13; 8:13 (θεωρέω) and John 11:45; Rev. 11:11 (θεάομαι), where the English word "witness" would be an appropriate translation; e.g., "Many of...*those who had witnessed* [οἱ... θεασάμενοι] the things which he had done" (John 11:45; my trans.). In the LXX, see, for instance, Judges 16:27 for the Philistine "onlookers" (οἱ θεωροῦντες) at Samson's "entertainment"; cf. Ps. 22:7 (21:8 in LXX) for the mocking audience of the Stricken One. Cf. Trites: "In other words, the context rules out the thought of spectators in an amphitheatre who watch the

contemporary Christian race. . ." (*Witness*, 221). Moffatt wants to include this idea as well as the more active idea of their witnessing to us (*Hebrews*, 193). (See Baugh, 120, footnote 32.)

[14] Baugh defends this conclusion by arguing:

> The meaning, "approved" for μαρτυρέω is given in the lexicons primarily for the idea of speaking well about someone (e.g., Luke 4:22); or in the passive for someone whose life or good conduct is "well attested" by the community (e.g., Acts 10:22), someone "of [good] repute" (Acts 6:3). However, the first use in Heb. 11:4 has an infinitive clause (ἐμαρτυρήθη εἶναι δίκαιος), which clearly shows that the author intends to identify the content of testimony being borne (as, e.g., Acts 10:43; cf. equivalent ὅτι clauses in Heb. 7:8 and 17). Hence the renderings "he was commended as a righteous man" (NIV; cf. ESV) or "he received approval as righteous" (NRSV) are not possible. The Greek word συνευδοκέω "approve" would have been used for this meaning; cf. Luke 11:48; Acts 8:1; and Rom. 1:32. The versions go off course even more in the second clause when they have God speak well of his offerings (NIV), approve the gifts, or even, "God commending him by accepting his gifts" (ESV). μαρτυρέω with ἐπί shows that God is "bearing witness to" or "attesting to" Abel's gift as being more valuable than Cain's because they are pointers to the greater sacrifice to come. The ἐπι clause specifies that element with regard to which testimony is borne. While μαρτυρέω + ἐπι is not found in the NT or LXX, parallel examples can be found elsewhere (e.g., Josephus, *A.J.* 3.59, 189 and 17.101; cf. *A.J.* 2.262 and 6.346 for μαρτυρία + ἐπί; and see μαρτύς + ἐπί in Philo, Spec. 2.252). (See Baugh, 123, footnote 43.)

[15] Baugh, 125.

[16] Although Enoch may not have known that, ultimately, the Lord's ministry would require two comings, he clearly knew that God

would come to earth to cleanse it from sin in conjunction with its reclamation.

[17] Ibid., 127.

[18] Ibid., 128.

[19] Ibid., 131.

[20] Geerhardus Vos, *The Teaching of Jesus Concerning the Kingdom of God and the Church* (Eugene: Wipf & Stock Publishers, 1998), 67–68.

[21] Adopting this position creates another problem. The Old Testament suggests that Moses left Egypt the first time out of fear for his life. Exodus 2:14 states that Moses was afraid when he learned that his secret about killing the Egyptian was known to all. Exodus 2:15 indicates that Pharaoh sought to kill Moses after hearing of Moses' action. Moses fled from Pharaoh and settled in the land of Midian. The apparent contradiction is evident. However, while the Old Testament text does say that Moses was afraid, it does not say that Moses was afraid of Pharaoh.

Chapter 10

Conclusion

N

o event in human history will have had the
amount of revelatory preparation as the
consummation of this age. That there is going to be
a catastrophic end to the world is sewn into the
fabric of human DNA. Hollywood has made
millions playing on this fear. Unfortunately, just as
those who heard the boy who cried wolf too often,
the world has grown dull of hearing.

However, as believers, we have everything we
need to be fully prepared to face that unparalleled
time of persecution by Satan and his Antichrist.
The same faith required to obtain God's salvation
from sin, the same faith required to live each day in

full dependency on God, the same faith to believe in the resurrection of those dead for four thousand years, the same faith to believe in the evacuation of the righteous from the earth, the same faith to believe that God loves us is the same faith necessary to face the Great Persecution--TRUTH.

Any fear of what may happen simply exposes our failure to allow the evidence of faith to control our emotions. God has promised in His Word to help us by ultimately delivering us into His temporal and eternal kingdoms. Every event during the seven years of Daniel's final week will be under God's sovereignty.

In Revelation 6:2, a description is given of a rider on a white horse. It is said of this rider, "it was given to him (ἐδόθη αὐτῷ). . ." This particular usage occurs twenty-two times in the Book of Revelation. David E. Aune, in his excellent commentary on this book, explains the verbal function in this sentence as a *passivum divinum*, "passive of divine activity."[1] Scholars recognize its usage, but do not agree on precisely what it means. Aune indicates, "The use of the divine passive does not of itself appear to indicate the positive or negative aspects of divine enablement envisaged."[2] Regarding this key sentence, G. K. Beale writes,

> That this first destructive rider is ultimately under the hand of God is apparent from the phrase ἐδόθη αὐτῷ ("it was given to him"), which is an authorization clause with God as the subject (as is clear from other uses of

Conclusion

the passive of δίδωμι ["give"] elsewhere in the book, e.g., 6:11; 7:2; 8:2–3; 9:1, 3, 5; 11:2–3; 12:14; repeatedly in ch. 13; cf. 17:17). The clause is used in commissioning both good and evil intermediary agents and is best understood in the specific sense of a divine authorization to perform a role rather than the more general idea of "permit, allow."[3]

Robert L. Thomas adds in contradistinction,

It [the crown] was given to him not as something he personally acquired or earned, but by permission of a higher authority to whom all beings are ultimately submissive. In Revelation *edothē* ("was given") speaks of divine permission for evil powers to carry out their wicked mission."[4]

So we are left with a choice. Does God permit or does He authorize the actions of the agent? Regardless of how one understands this unique phrase, the fact is this: God determines what is going to happen. Every event is under His sovereign control. Whether He indirectly allows or directly authorizes it, we must trust that His way is best. We are left with one choice. Will we trust and obey?

We do not have to understand *why* God will allow the Great Persecution to occur, but we must be prepared doctrinally to respond with appropriate truth when it does. For then and only then can we expect to receive the commendation, "Well done, you servant of 'great faith.'"

---

[1] David E. Aune, *Revelation 6–16*, *WBC* 52b (Nashville: Thomas Nelson Publishers, 1998), 394–395.

[2] Ibid., 395.

[3] G. K. Beale, *The Book of Revelation: A Commentary on the Greek Text* (Grand Rapids, Mich.; Carlisle, Cumbria: W.B. Eerdmans; Paternoster Press, 1999), 377.

[4] Robert L. Thomas, *Revelation 1–7: An Exegetical Commentary* (Chicago: Moody Press, 1992), 423.